WINNING WAYS AT BRIDGE

WINNING WAYS AT BRIDGE

RHODA LEDERER AND DAVID GRIFFITHS

CollinsWillow
An Imprint of HarperCollins*Publishers*

First published in 1987 by Unwin® Paperbacks
Reprinted 1989

Revised edition published in 1993 by
Collins Willow
an imprint of HarperCollins*Publishers*, London

**A CIP catalogue record for this book
is available from the British Library**

ISBN 0 00 218439 7

Set in Palatino
Printed and bound in Great Britain
by Cox & Wyman Ltd

Contents

Preface

This book is designed to complement the others in the series, which concentrate mainly on teaching the Acol bidding system. It sets out to give the improved player a wider view of what it really takes to tackle a hand from beginning to end.

From the beginning, of course, means starting with the bidding. Each chapter starts with a brief run-down on the principles of the correct Acol bidding, after which you are asked to plan the bidding of individual hands, in the light of what your partner or the opponents have bid. Having arrived at the right contract, you are shown two hands, your own and dummy, and asked to plan the play.

In the paragraph on planning, the authors have tried to lead you towards the way your thoughts should run – how many losers you have between the two hands, how you might dispose of them, and how many tricks you could expect to make if all goes well. The next paragraph deals with the actual play, and if anything unexpectedly horrible occurs, how you will have to rethink your plan to cope with it.

The final paragraph on each hand, headed 'Postscript', explains the reasons why you should choose the line you did, and the likely outcome, or any other points of interest.

In the case of the defensive hands you are shown your own hand and told what the bidding has been against you. If you are on declarer's left you will have to choose the opening lead and, if on his right, work out how you will continue the defence when you have to take an active part.

This book is intended for more than just reading. If that's all you do with it, it will do your bridge no good at all because it *is* meant to teach you winning ways! Look at each hand, read the questions, cover the answers and really try to work out what you should do before you look to see if you were right. If you got it wrong, make sure you understand why, and that you won't make the same mistake again! Used in this way, you are guaranteed to turn out a better bridge player than you were before you started!

CHAPTER 1

Bidding and Play of Balanced Hands

A balanced hand is one with suits of fairly equal length. Four cards in one suit and three in each of the others (a 4-3-3-3 shape) is the most balanced hand but 4-4-3-2 is also balanced. Many balanced hands are played in no-trump contracts. It often pays to bid no-trumps also on a 5-3-3-2 shape if the 5-card suit is a minor, but with a 5-card major it is usually (but by no means always) better to bid the long suit.

Assessing the strength of the hand

Most players use the Milton Work point count of ace = 4, king = 3, queen = 2, jack = 1. You need at least 12 points to open the bidding and at least 6 to reply if partner has made an opening bid. When you and your partner both have balanced hands you will probably try to play the contract in no-trumps; the level you choose will depend on how many points you have in the combined hands. With average luck 23 points in the *combined* hands will make 2NT (eight tricks). If you have more than this, for example 25-26 points, you should try to be in a game contract; if less, you should try to stop the bidding at the earliest opportunity.

The opening bid of 1NT

Bridge players divide into those who believe that the opening bid of 1NT should be strong (15-17 or 16-18 points, or even stronger) and those who believe it should be weak (12-14 or 13-15 points). The strong no-trump is sound but easy to play against; the weak no-trump is more risky but creates problems for the opponents. The weak no-trump is excellent for duplicate bridge but at rubber bridge it is probably best not to take up an entrenched attitude, but be willing to play whatever partner wants. The important thing is to agree the exact strength of the opening 1NT bid with partner and stick to it like glue.

Some players use the 'variable NT', 12-14 points not vulnerable and 15-17 points vulnerable. Any of these no-trump ranges may be used in the standard British bidding system, ACOL, on which all the bidding in this book is based.

The play of the cards by declarer

After the opening lead has been made, dummy's cards go down on the table and declarer plays both his and dummy's cards. He must assess the number of the tricks the combined hands will make. There will probably be some certain tricks, for example aces (or kings with aces), but declarer will seldom make his contract by simply playing out top tricks. He will usually have to develop extra tricks as described below.

One way of making extra tricks is to play on suits containing *good intermediate cards*. For example with ♠10-4-2 in one hand and ♠Q-J-9-3 in the other, declarer can make two tricks if he keeps leading the suit to force out the opponents' ace and king.

Another way of making extra tricks is to play on *long suits* until the opponents have no cards left in them and your remaining low cards will take tricks. For example, ♠A-2 in declarer's hand opposite ♠K-3 in dummy can make only two tricks and ♠A-2 … ♠K-4-3 or even ♠A-2 … ♠K-5-4-3 is worth only two tricks, but ♠A-2 opposite ♠K-6-5-4-3 may make extra tricks because of the length; thus if declarer plays the ace, crosses to the king and then plays a third spade, he will lose the third trick, but the opponents may have no more spades left and there will be two low spades left in dummy that can take tricks later. Declarer would be lucky to find opponents with exactly three spades each, and if one opponent had four spades and the other had two, declarer would have to lose two tricks in the suit to set up one extra winner.

A third way to make extra tricks is to take advantage of the position of opponents' high cards, ie, *to finesse*. For example, with ◊4-3-2 ... ◊K-Q-5 lead the two and if your left-hand opponent plays low, play the queen. If this holds the trick, return to your own hand by leading some other suit and play the three towards the king. If your left-hand opponent holds the ace you will take two tricks in the suit. With ◊5-4-3 ... ◊A-Q-2 you could lead a low card and try the queen, hoping your left-hand opponent holds the king. With ◊5-4-3 ... ◊A-Q-10 you could lead low towards the ten first, and if this loses to the jack, you could return to your own hand later and lead low towards the queen next time, hoping that at least one of the missing honours was with the left-hand opponent; this is known as 'playing for split honours'.

Blocking the opponents' suit

When you are declarer in a no-trump contract and the opponents lead their long suits, it will pay you to hold up your high cards to break communications between defenders' hands. Thus with A-x-x opposite x-x in dummy you would hold up twice and win the third round. Similarly you could hold up a king if the ace had already been played. Also, with A-x-x opposite K-x it is often correct to duck the first round, unless, of course, you wanted to save the king as an entry or there was a more dangerous suit to which the opponents could switch.

It is often helpful to use the rule of seven when you have only one guard in the suit led. Count the number of cards you hold in that suit between your two hands, subtract the total from 7, and the answer will be the number of times you need to duck. The rule assumes that the lead is from a 5-card suit.

♠ A K 8
♡ A 8 5
◊ K 7 2
♣ Q 9 8 2

Deal 1. Assume that, at some stage in the rubber, you hold the hand shown on the left. What is your opening bid?

The hand contains 16 points (4 for each ace, 3 for each king and 2 for the queen). Its 4-3-3-3 shape is the most balanced possible and you would normally plan to bid no-trumps rather than a suit. If you have agreed with partner to play a strong no-trump your hand is suitable for a 1NT opening bid. If you have agreed to play the weak no-trump, or the variable no-trump and you happen not to be vulnerable, you must open 1♣, your only 4-card suit, and rebid 1NT.

The bidding	*You*	*Partner*
Strong no-trump	1NT	3NT
Weak no-trump	1♣	1♡
	1NT	3NT

Partner's hand.

♠ Q 7 3
♡ K Q 9 4
◇ A 9 5
♣ J 10 5

Twenty-eight points in the combined hands is ample for game, which is worth trying on a combined 25, though well below the slam level, which requires about 33 combined points when the hands are balanced.

Your partner was right, therefore, to bid 3NT only, as you score no more for bidding and making 4NT or 5NT than you do for 3NT with overtricks.

North leads the ♠J against West's contract of 3NT. Plan the play.

♠ A K 8	N	♠ Q 7 3
♡ A 8 5	W E	♡ K Q 9 4
◇ K 7 2	S	◇ A 9 5
♣ Q 9 8 2		♣ J 10 5

Planning: Whenever playing a no-trump contract, and before playing a single card from dummy (a) look for the danger suit, ie opponent's long suit, (b) count your certain winners and (c) make your plans. A common mistake in bridge is to play one of dummy's cards quickly, before planning the hand, and to find out later that it was the wrong thing to do. However, this is an easy hand. No suit is particularly dangerous because, although North led a spade, probably from a long suit headed by a sequence (such as ♠J-10-9-x-x), you have three stoppers in the suit. Your certain winners are three spades, three hearts and two diamonds. You have good intermediate cards in clubs which will provide two tricks once the ace and the king have been forced out.

The play: Win the opening lead with a high spade. Play a club to the jack or ten. If it wins, continue clubs. If it loses, win the lead in whatever suit the opponents return and continue clubs to force out the remaining high honour. Win the lead again, cash the club winners, the remaining high cards in spades and diamonds, and the ♡A-K-Q. If the opponents' hearts are three in each hand, dummy will make a fourth heart trick, giving you eleven tricks in all.

Postscript: You can't rely on four heart tricks to make your contract. The opponents' hearts will split 3-3 less than half the time (see Appendix). When playing the hearts for overtricks as above, avoid the mistake of playing the ♡K and ♡Q first and then getting stuck in the wrong hand with the ♡A with no entry back to dummy.

♠ A Q 8 *Deal 2.* Your right-hand opponent deals and
♡ J 4 2 passes. What do you bid on this hand?
◇ 9 6 5
♣ A Q 4 3

Like the first hand, this is balanced, but there are now only 13 high card points. It is suitable for a weak no-trump opening bid; guards in three suits are all that are required for the weak no-trump – the weakness in diamonds must be risked. Players of the strong no-trump have to open 1♣ and rebid 1NT. With a balanced hand of the wrong strength for the no-trump you have agreed to play, you can often describe your hand by bidding a suit and rebidding in no-trumps. There are, however, some important exceptions (Deals 9 and 10).

The bidding	You	Partner
Strong no-trump	1♣	1◇
	1NT	3NT
Weak no-trump	1NT	3NT

Partner has 14 high card points and a 5-card suit (see below). He is correct to respond only 1◊, not 2◊, a jump shift which is reserved for hands on which not only is a game certain but there is a possibility of a slam. He can safely respond 1◊ because when a player opens the bidding with one of a suit (not NT) he guarantees a rebid. When partner has heard the rebid he will have a much better picture of opener's hand and can judge the final contract.

In both sequences shown above partner is right to go for 3NT instead of persisting with his diamond suit. Game in diamonds needs eleven tricks, which cannot be made on these hands. The length in diamonds will be useful in a no-trump contract, as we shall see.

North leads the ♣J against West's contract of 3NT. Plan the play.

Planning: As declarer, the first thing you should do is try to work out what cards are now marked as being in the leader's hand. Here the ♣J is almost certainly from the top of a sequence such as ♣J-10-9-x-x, or from an internal sequence such as ♣K-J-10-9-x. Fortunately, with the lead coming up to your ♣A-Q you have two certain stops in the suit, whoever has the ♣K, but clubs are clearly your danger. Count your other certain tricks – one spade, two hearts, and two diamonds, making seven in all. You need, therefore, to develop two more tricks. You have a long diamond suit, of which only five cards are missing. If these split 3-2 you merely have to play three rounds of the suit and you will then have the last two diamonds left as winners in dummy.

The play: Win the first trick with the ♣Q (or the ♣A if South plays the ♣K). Lead the ◊5 and put on the ◊2 from dummy; you have to lose one diamond and you might as well lose it now. The opponents will win and will probably return a club. Regain the lead and play off ◊A-K to draw the outstanding cards in the suit. Cash the two diamonds left in dummy, and your other top tricks.

Postscript: The suggested line of play will succeed about two times out of three, but will fail if the opponents' diamonds split 4-1 or 5-0. A table of odds as to how the missing cards divide is given in the Appendix. You need not learn these odds but merely note that if an even number of cards is missing they probably will not split evenly, but if an odd number of cards is missing they will probably split as evenly as possible. Thus on Deal 1 the six cards would probably not split 3-3 but on Deal 2 the five missing diamonds probably *would* split 3-2.

♠ A 8 5   *Deal 3.* What is your opening bid on this hand?
♡ A 8 4
◇ 6 5 4
♣ A K J 2

This balanced hand should be considered for a no-trump contract. Lack of good intermediate cards is a poor feature but the hand has strength in its long suit and should take several tricks. Sixteen high card points are about right for a strong no-trump opening bid and this is probably the best way of describing the hand, even though the strong no-trump normally guarantees a stop in each suit. Players of the weak no-trump should open 1♣ and rebid 1NT.

The bidding	*You*	*Partner*
Strong no-trump	1NT	3NT
Weak no-trump	1♣	1◇
	1NT	3NT

Over your opening bid of 1♣ partner conveniently bid 1◇, your weak suit, so you could rebid 1NT with confidence. Even if partner had responded 1♡ or 1♠ you should still rebid 1NT (risking the weakness in diamonds) because you can't *rebid* clubs with less than five or raise partner's suit with less than 4-card support.

Partner's hand	♠ Q 4 3 2
	♡ 7 2
	◇ A Q 10 9
	♣ Q 6 4

In the sequence 1NT – 3NT he might have explored a possible fit in spades, particularly because his hearts are weak and a suit contract might, therefore, have been safer. Ways of exploring a major suit fit after a 1NT opening bid are described on p.31. However, partner knew you had enough strength for game and 3NT was not an unreasonable bid. In the second sequence partner knew you lacked a biddable major as you could have shown it over 1◊, so 3NT looks an obvious contract.

North leads the ♡K against West's contract of 3NT. Plan the play.

♠ A 8 5		♠ Q 4 3 2
♡ A 8 4	**N**	♡ 7 2
◊ 6 5 4	**W E**	◊ A Q 10 9
♣ A K J 2	**S**	♣ Q 6 4

Planning: There are seven certain tricks, four in clubs and one in each of the other suits, and you must plan to make your contract by making two extra tricks from diamonds. You can do this by taking a deep finesse in diamonds, playing for split honours in the suit. The danger suit is hearts; if you play the ♡A the first time and take a losing diamond finesse into the South hand, he will return a heart to his partner's established suit. You must, therefore, break communications between the opponents' hands by holding up the ♡A (rule of seven).

The play: Hold up the ♡A until the third round, lead a low diamond and finesse the ◊9 into the South hand. If it loses to the ◊J and a spade comes back, don't risk allowing North in with the ♠K, but go up with the ♠A and lead another diamond, this time finessing the ◊10. If this wins, don't cash the ◊A, as North may have started with four to the ◊K, but come back to hand with a club and lead a low diamond again. This should ensure three tricks in diamonds provided South did not start with both ◊K and ◊J. It remains only to cash the diamonds and the high club in dummy before coming back to hand for the remaining club tricks.

Postscript: What if South has four hearts and is able to lead one when he gets in, despite your having held up the ♡A until the third round? This won't hurt you, as if South has four hearts North also has only four and you can't lose more than three tricks in the suit. The hold up has everything to gain and nothing to lose.

♠ A 5 4   *Deal 4.* What is your opening bid on this hand?
♡ A K 5 2
◊ 9 5 3
♣ K Q 2

Another balanced 16-point hand suitable for opening 1NT if the strong no-trump has been agreed. Players of the weak no-trump should open one of the biddable suit (hearts) and rebid no-trumps at the minimum level, ie, 1NT over a one-level response, or 2NT over a 2-level response.

The bidding	*You*	*Partner*
Strong no-trump	1NT	3NT
Weak no-trump	1♡	2◊
	2NT	3NT

In the strong no-trump sequence, partner (see hand below) merely added his points to yours and bid the game. In the weak no-trump sequence partner's first bid, a response at the two-level, could have been made on as few as 8 points. Your rebid of 2NT, therefore, guaranteed 15 or 16 points as you need 23 points in the combined hands for 2NT. Having more than his minimum, partner was able to raise you to 3NT.

North leads the ♠K against West's contract of 3NT. Plan the play.

♠ A 5 4		♠ 8 3
♡ A K 5 2	N	♡ J 9 2
◊ 9 5 3	W E	◊ A Q 10 8 2
♣ K Q 2	S	♣ A 7 4

Planning: Three top clubs, two top hearts and two aces make seven certain tricks. Clearly the extra tricks will have to come from diamonds. The danger suit is spades in which you only have one stop, so the ♠A will have to be held up, and diamond finesses will have to be taken into the South hand after he has been run out of spades.

The play: Hold up the ♠A twice (to block the suit). Win the third round. Lead the ◊9 and if North plays low, play the ◊2 from dummy. If South wins with the ◊J and returns a heart, go up with the ♡A so that you don't let North into the lead. Now lead a low diamond towards dummy; even if North shows out, you will lose only one more diamond trick to South and you will have enough tricks for the contract. Go up, of course, with the ♡K if South persists with this suit.

Postscript: This is another illustration of the hold-up, to break communications between opponents' hands. Again one has to avoid playing suits that contain certain tricks and to concentrate on the suit in which work has to be done. Even if South started with both ◊K and ◊J the contract is safe, provided North is kept out of the lead. Declarer ducked twice here because he could not be sure the lead was from a 5-card suit. He had to make certain of his contract, whether spades were 6-2 or 5-3.

The rule of seven worked well again here, with A-x-x opposite x-x, however, it is by no means completely infallible and is only intended as a guide.

♠ 5 3   *Deal 5.* What is your opening bid on this hand?
♡ A Q J 10 9
◊ A 6 2
♣ A K J

There are two reasons for not bidding 1NT. Firstly, you are too strong even for a 16-18 point no-trump; secondly, you have a strong 5-card major suit.

The obvious opening is 1♡, and if partner can bid at all, you make a jump shift (forcing to game) or else bid game direct, on the next round.

The bidding	*You*	*Partner*
	1♡	1♠
	3NT	

Spades are just what you wanted partner to bid, as it protects the weakness in your own hand. Although the hearts are rebiddable, it looks as if 3NT will be the best contract and so you have no hesitation in bidding it direct.

Partner's hand   ♠ A 8 4 2
                        ♡ 6 3
                        ◊ K 9 4
                        ♣ 5 4 3 2

Some players would respond 1NT with these cards, merely to show a weak balanced hand (about 6-8 points). This is a mistake when there is a 4-card major suit that can be shown at the one-level; opener may have five hearts and four spades, and if responder doesn't show the spade suit, opener may not be strong enough to go to 2♠ over 1NT, so the vital 4-4 major fit will be lost. It costs nothing to respond 1♠ because, although this response could also be made on quite strong hands, its minimum is just 6 points (like the minimum for 1NT), and it is the minimum that partner must assume when making his rebid. Also, on the inferior sequence 1♡-1NT-3NT the strong hand would be exposed as dummy, possibly making it easier for the opponents to defend.

North leads ◊Q against West's contract of 3NT. Plan the play.

♠ 5 3
♡ A Q J 10 9
◊ A 6 2
♣ A K J
             N
      W   E
             S
                   ♠ A 8 4 2
                   ♡ 6 3
                   ◊ K 9 4
                   ♣ 5 4 3 2

Planning: It could well be a fatal mistake to duck the opening lead on this hand because it is the spade suit, not the diamonds, where the main danger lies. If you duck the ◊Q, the opponents could switch to a spade and, once the ♠A has been forced out, you are wide open in the suit. The certain winners are one spade, two diamonds and two clubs, so you need four heart tricks to make the contract.

The play: Go up with the ◊K and lead a low heart to the ♡9. If it loses to North's ♡K the heart suit is set up. If it wins, play the ♡A at trick 3 and continue with the ♡Q. The opponents can win with the ♡K whenever they wish, but you need only four heart tricks for your contract and it is essential to set up the suit before your vital stoppers in the others suits are played.

Postscript: Don't make the mistake of going over, at trick 3, to dummy's ♠A to repeat an apparently successful heart finesse. The ♠A is far too valuable a card to release at this stage; if you do so in order to take a second heart finesse, North may win the trick (yes, the defence can hold up high cards too!) and the opponents will then cash spade after spade after spade.

CHAPTER 2

More Balanced Hands

Opening bids on weak balanced hands

Balanced hands of 12-14 points can be awkward to bid because of the difficulty of finding a safe rebid. For example, with

♠ Q 10 4
♡ A J 5 4
♢ Q 10 3
♣ A 4 2

it would be wrong to open 1♡ because, if partner responds 2♣ or 2♢, you must not rebid your hearts on only a 4-card suit, and you can't rebid 2NT or three of partner's suit because these contracts require 23 points in the combined hands and, at this stage, partner has guaranteed only eight. A simple solution is to use the weak no-trump. By opening 1NT there is no need to find a rebid because you have described the hand completely. Players of the strong no-trump try to solve the problem by opening a 'prepared' 1♣, which can be done on three cards to an honour, and rebidding 1NT. If, on the hand shown above, you opened a 'prepared' 1♣ and partner responded 1♡, it would be correct to raise him to 2♡, but if he bid 1♢ or 1♠ it would be wrong to show the hearts because partner would think that, as you bid clubs first, you had more clubs than hearts. When you open a 'prepared' minor suit you *must* rebid no-trumps unless partner happens to bid your 4-card suit. This 1♣ opening, however, often causes more problems than it solves, as it lets the opponents into the bidding very cheaply.

Responses to 1NT on balanced hands

If partner opens 1NT and you have a balanced hand, you should either pass or raise his no-trump contract. Assume that partner has the *minimum* of points needed for his bid and simply add your points to his. If the combined points add up to less than 23, you should pass; on a combined total of 23-24 points bid 2NT invitationally (partner will go on to 3NT if he has a maximum); on a combined total of 25-30 points, bid 3NT. On a combined total of 31-32 points bid 4NT, inviting partner to bid 6NT on a maximum; with a combined total of 33 points, bid 6NT direct.

Similarly, if partner opens 2NT, showing a balanced hand of 20-22 points, you could raise to 3NT on 5-10 points (or even on 4-10), bid 6NT with 13 points or bid 4NT with 11-12 points, a quantitative bid inviting partner to go to 6NT if he is maximum.

There is one other, less well-known, alternative – a direct raise of partner's 1NT or 2NT opening bid to 5NT. This tells partner to bid 6NT even with a minimum and to bid 7NT on a maximum. Responder makes the bid when he knows that 6NT is safe and that, if opener has a maximum, there will be at least 37 points in the combined hands.

More hints on play

In the play of no-trump contracts we have already seen that declarer must count the certain winners, look for the danger suit, and make his plans before playing a card. Often one opponent is more dangerous than the other and declarer may be able to keep him out of the lead by *blocking plays* such as the hold-up of high cards to break communications between the opponents' hands.

To establish a long suit, declarer often has to lose the lead to one or other of the opponents and is sometimes able to choose which one to allow into the lead. When the lead must be lost to both opponents, it is best to let the dangerous opponent in first, whilst there are still stoppers in the danger suits, and to allow the other opponent in later, when he has no winners to make.

On some hands there is a choice of ways in which to make extra tricks, for example by playing for suits to split, or by taking

finesses in other suits. The skill in playing these contracts lies in
making the most of all the chances.

♠ A 5 3   *Deal 6.* What is your opening bid on this hand?
♡ K J 9 5
◇ A J 6
♣ A 8 3

This 17-point balanced hand is ideal for players of the strong no-
trump and, having opened 1NT, they can leave it to partner to
make the final decision. Players of the weak no-trump should
open 1♡ and rebid in no-trumps; if partner responds at the one-
level, guaranteeing only 6 points, then the correct rebid is 2NT, as
you know you have at least 23 points between you. If he responds
2♣ or 2◇, guaranteeing 8 points, the correct rebid is 3NT.

The bidding	*You*	*Partner*
Strong no-trump	1NT	NB
Weak no-trump	1♡	1♠
	2NT	NB

In the strong no-trump sequence, partner's response will depend
on the exact strength of the opening bid. If it shows 15-17 points,
the combined holding could be only 22 points, and partner is right
to pass. If you have agreed that 1NT shows 16-18 points, he should
bid 2NT, inviting you to go to game on a maximum, for you will
then have 25 points between you. This illustrates how important it
is for the partnership to agree exactly the strength of the no-trump
opening bid, and to stick to it.

   In the second sequence partner is right to reply 1♠ (see Deal 5).
When you rebid 2NT, a limit-bid, he has only one point to spare
and no long suit, and can pass.

North leads the ◇K against West's no-trump contract. Plan the play.

```
              ♠ A 5 3        ┌─────┐    ♠ K Q 7 6
          □   ♡ K J 9 5      │  N  │    ♡ 10 8 4
              ◇ A J 6      W │     │ E  ◇ 8 7 2
              ♣ A 8 3        │  S  │    ♣ Q 5 2
                             └─────┘
```

(handwritten: Show 4 card major rather than bid 1NT.)

Planning: Firstly, what is that lead from? Top-of-sequence leads are popular (p.135) but North can't have ◊K-Q-J-x because you have the jack yourself. He could have a near sequence, such as ◊K-Q-10-9 or ◊K-Q-10-9-x, so diamonds seem to be the dangerous suit. The certain winners are three spade tricks and two minor suit aces. You may be able to make the ♣Q if North has the king but extra tricks will have to come from hearts; if South has the ♡Q you can always make three heart tricks by leading them through him.

What use should one make of the spades? It is a mistake to play off ♠A-K-Q early on, hoping for a 3-3 split; they either split evenly (unlikely) or they don't. There is nothing you can do to improve your prospects in spades but there is urgent work to be done in hearts and the spades will provide useful entries to dummy for heart finesses.

The play: Duck the first diamond! This is known as the Bath Coup (see below). If North falls for it and continues with the suit he will give you two diamond tricks. Being brighter than that he switches to a spade, so you win in dummy and lead the ♡8. If this holds you lead the ♡10 and play the ♡9 from your hand if South plays low again, to retain the lead in dummy to lead hearts a third time. You will now be able to make three heart tricks, even if South started with four cards in the suit, and will still have time to try for extra tricks in the black suits later.

Postscript: The Bath Coup, the duck of the first trick with A-J-x when the left-hand opponent has led the K from K-Q, is a simple stratagem borrowed from whist.

The heart suit was played in such a way as to retain the lead in dummy for successive finesses against South.

♠ A J 8　　　　　*Deal 7.* What is your opening bid on this hand?
♡ A K 5 3
◊ K 7 4 2
♣ A Q

This 21-point hand is too strong to open 1NT but is ideal for a 2NT opening bid, showing a balanced hand of 20-22 points. The club suit is a possible danger but a club opening lead will come up to the ♣A-Q, so giving you two stops in the suit.

The bidding	You	Partner
	2NT	3NT

Partner (see hand below) knows that you have a maximum of 29 points between you and that this is not enough for a slam. It is, therefore, correct to settle for game. He might have explored for a possible 4-4 fit in spades by way of the Baron convention (see p.70), but he settled instead for the more straightforward bid of 3NT. There is no weakness take-out of 2NT except by way of the Flint conventional bids described later, or by red suit transfer bids. Although he has a strong minor suit, there is no point in trying to play in clubs as 3NT will surely be easier to make than 5♣. The clubs will take tricks in a no-trump contract and no-trumps scores more.

North leads the ◇6 against West's contract of 3NT. Plan the play.

♠ A J 8	N	♠ 6 5 3 2
♡ A K 5 3		♡ 10 7
◇ K 7 4 2	W E	◇ A 5
♣ A Q	S	♣ K 10 9 6 2

Planning: The lead could be from a long suit, such as five diamonds to the queen. With one sure spade trick, two hearts and two diamonds, declarer needs four tricks from clubs. The problem on the hand is the shortage of entries to dummy. It's unlikely that the clubs will split 3-3 and the ♣J must be forced out at the first opportunity.

The play: Win the first trick with the ◇K, preserving the ◇A in dummy. Play the ♣A and follow it with the ♣Q, overtaking with the ♣K in dummy. Continue with the ♣10 and, if necessary, the ♣9 to force out the ♣J. Now you still have the ◇A as an entry to the last club on the table, so the contract will succeed provided the clubs are not 5-1 or 6-0.

Postscript: Inexperienced players will go down on this hand by making one of three possible mistakes. The first is to play the ◇A on the first round, removing dummy's entry to the club suit. The second is to play a low diamond from both hands at trick one, because the opponents will continue with a second diamond to force out the ◊A. The third possible error is to misplay the clubs; if declarer plays the ♣A, the ♣Q, and then enters dummy with the ◊A and plays the ♣K, there is no way of making the contract when the ♣J does not fall.

♠ A J 7 6   *Deal 8*. What is your opening bid on this hand?
♡ K Q J
◊ A 7 4
♣ A 7 2

Nineteen points are too many for an opening bid of 1NT, even for the strong no-trump brigade. The hand has to be opened 1♠ and rebid strongly. Game is certain if partner can find some response but, if he can't reply to your opening bid, a one-level contract will be enough.

The bidding   *You*   *Partner*
                     1♠   2◊
                     3NT

Knowing that your partner has at least 8 points, you can immediately bid game.

Partner's 2◊ response is minimum (see below). He has 8 points and a 5-card suit, but the ♣J is hardly worth a point, guarded as it is by only one other card in the suit. However, the alternative response of 1NT is unattractive as it is likely to result in the weak hand playing the contract with the strong hand exposed on table as dummy.

North leads the ♣K against West's contract of 3NT. Plan the play.

	N	♠ 10 5 4
♠ A J 7 6		♡ A 5 4
♡ K Q J	W E	◊ K 10 5 3 2
◊ A 7 4		♣ J 3
♣ A 7 2	S	

Planning: The lead of the ♣K is probably from a strong suit such as ♣K-Q-10-9 or ♣K-Q-10-9-x, and it finds your weakness straightaway. You will have to try to block the suit by holding up the ♣A for two rounds. Your certain winners are one spade, three hearts and one club so you will need four tricks from diamonds.

You will have to hope for a 3-2 split in this suit and you must avoid losing a diamond trick to the danger hand (North).

The play: Duck the ♣K; when North continues with the ♣Q, duck this too, and take the third club trick with the ♣A. Play the ◊A and then a low diamond from your hand. If North produces an honour, win with the ◊K and lead another diamond to clear the suit.

If North plays low on the second diamond, play the ◊10 from dummy, allowing South to win. When South makes his diamond trick he will probably switch to a spade if he has no clubs left. Win the spade lead with the ♠A and cash the winning hearts and diamonds.

Postscript: The suggested line of play succeeds against a 3-2 diamond break provided North did not start with ◊Q-J-x. It does not matter if South turns up with a fourth club because North will then have only four clubs and you can't lose more than three club tricks.

♠ K 5 3   *Deal 9*. What is your opening bid on this hand?
♡ K Q J 4
◊ J 9 3
♣ K 4 3

This balanced hand of 13 points is suitable for an opening bid of 1NT if you have agreed to play the weak no-trump. If you play the strong no-trump, you should open 1♣ and rebid 1NT, except when partner responds 1♡, when you should raise his opening bid to 2♡.

The bidding	*You*	*Partner*
Strong no-trump	1♣	1◊
	1NT	3NT
Weak no-trump	1NT	3NT

In each sequence partner knows you have a balanced hand of about 13 points, so he raises to 3NT. There is no point in persisting with the diamond suit; nine tricks in no-trumps are much more likely than eleven tricks in diamonds.

North leads the ♣6 against West's contract of 3NT. South wins with the ♠J and returns the ♣8 to your ♣K. Plan the play.

♠ K 5 3	N	♠ A 7 2
♡ K Q J 4	W E	♡ 6 5
◊ J 9 3	S	◊ A Q 10 6 4
♣ K 4 3		♣ A 7 2

Planning: North has probably led from a long suit such as ♠Q-10-x-x-x so spades are dangerous. You have only four certain tricks in the black suits and, if you can't make all five diamond tricks, you will need a heart trick as well. Which red suit should you tackle first? If you play on diamonds and lose to South's king, he will force out your ♠A and North may get in later with the ♡A and cash his spade winners. However, if you try the hearts first, the opponent who has the ♡A will force out your ♠A, but you will still have time to finesse the diamonds against North, to ensure that he doesn't get the lead.

The play: Duck the first spade (rule of seven) and take the second with your ♠K. Play the ♡K. If this wins, don't be tempted to continue with the ♡Q; South may have started with ♡A-10-9-x-x and will then force out your ♡J. Having secured one heart trick, switch to diamonds, leading ◊J and finessing North for the ◊K. If this loses to South, you still have your spade stop and the diamonds are established.

Postscript: Playing on the short heart suit before the long diamond suit was necessary to ensure that the lead was lost first to the dangerous opponent. The diamonds could be played later in such a way as to keep the danger hand out of the lead. Turning back to the play of the spades, the blocking play still operates when you have two guards in the suit, *provided that you don't fear a switch to a more dangerous suit.*

♠ A 9 8	*Deal 10.* What is your opening bid on this hand?
♡ A K 8 5	
◊ K 9 4	
♣ 9 3 2	

If you play the weak no-trump you will open 1NT. Should partner respond 4NT (a quantitative bid) you will accept his invitation to bid 6NT as you have a maximum for your opening bid. Don't be alarmed – partner knew your maximum was 14 points when you opened a (weak) NT.

Players of the strong no-trump have to open with a 'prepared' minor and to rebid 1NT. A prepared minor should guarantee at least three cards to an honour in the suit bid, but nowadays, if unable to open 1NT, many would prefer 1♣ to 1◊. Partner now bids 2♠, a jump shift, showing a strong hand and guaranteeing game, with some hope of a slam. You would have bid 1NT over 1♠ so you must now bid 2NT over 2♠. Partner continues with 4NT, which is quantitative, not a slam convention, as you have not agreed a suit. You now bid 6NT as you were maximum for your previous bids.

The bidding	You	Partner
Strong no-trump	1♣	2♠
	2NT	4NT
	6NT	
Weak no-trump	1NT	4NT
	6NT	

With 19 points (see below) partner must make a jump shift over 1♣, forcing to game. In both sequences opener has shown a balanced hand of 12-14 points and responder bids 4NT to invite 6NT, knowing that, if his partner is maximum, there will be 33 points in the combined hands.

North leads the ♣8 against West's contract of 6NT. South beats dummy's ♣10 with the ♣K and returns a low club. Plan the play.

```
        ♠ A 9 8          N          ♠ K Q 3 2
        ♡ A K 8 5                   ♡ Q 7 2
        ◊ K 9 4      W       E      ◊ A J
        ♣ 9 3 2          S          ♣ A Q J 10
```

Planning: There are now three certain club tricks, two diamonds, three hearts and three spades, so one more trick must be found somewhere. Possibilities for making an extra trick are (a) a 3-3 split in spades, (b) a 3-3 split in hearts or (c) a finesse of the ◊J.

Unfortunately you can't try all these chances because if you first try for the spade and heart splits and they don't succeed, you will have no entries back to your hand to try the diamond finesse. To manage diamonds, two entries are needed in declarer's hand, one to lead a low diamond to the ◊J and another to get back after the ◊A has been cashed in order to cash the ◊K. One must choose, therefore, between the diamond finesse (50 per cent chance) and the 3-3 heart split (a 36 per cent chance).

The play: Cash the remaining clubs, throwing a heart from hand. Try for the spade split (North shows out on the third round), enter your hand with a heart and lead a low diamond to the ◊J. If this wins, cash the ◊A and return to hand with a heart to cash the ◊K.

Postscript: The contract goes down only when the club finesse fails, the spades don't split and the ◊Q is with South, so the simple line of play suggested has more than an 80 per cent chance of success.

The process of evolution works even on bidding systems, and the 'prepared' 1◊ has dropped virtually into disuse. This poses a problem for players of the strong NT who pick up the West hand above. Just one more argument in favour of the weak NT!

CHAPTER 3

Suit Responses to One No-trump

With an *unbalanced hand* that is *weak* in high card points, responder should bid two of his long suit (2◊, 2♡, 2♠) and opener *must* pass; the response of two of a suit to either a weak or strong no-trump is a *weak take-out* and could be made on no points at all.

With a *strong* unbalanced hand, responder has to bid more strongly, at the three-level or above. A response of three of a suit is forcing; if made in a major suit it shows at least a 5-card suit and asks opener to raise the suit with three or more cards in it, or to bid 3NT with a doubleton in the suit.

A response of 2♣ to opener's 1NT is used to explore a possible 4-4 fit in a major suit. This is the *Stayman* convention; the 2♣ response is artificial and forcing. It does *not* show a club suit but an interest in one or both of the major suits. Opener must now bid his 4-card major suit if he has one or else bid 2◊, denying a 4-card major. Before bidding 2♣ (Stayman) responder must work out what to do if opener responds 2◊ or the 'wrong' major suit. For example if partner opens a weak no-trump and you hold:

(a) ♠ K Q 6 3	(b) ♠ K 8 4 3	(c) ♠ J 10 6 3 2	(d) ♠ K 8 4 3
♡ K J 4 2	♡ K 7 4 2	♡ J 7 5 3	♡ K 9 2
◊ K 9 6	◊ Q 6 5	◊ 8 7	◊ K 8 3
♣ 7 5	♣ 7 5	♣ 7 5	♣ Q 10 3

On (a) bid 2♣; if partner bids a major suit, raise to four, and if he replies 2◊ you can bid 2NT. On (b) you must pass because if partner replies 2◊ to a 2♣ enquiry you have nowhere to go, not being strong enough to rebid 2NT. On (c) you can try 2♣ despite your weak hand; if partner has no 4-card major you can retreat to 2♠. Hand (d) is so balanced that a raise to 2NT is preferable to using Stayman.

If the player who opened 1NT has *both* major suits he should show the hearts first in response to a Stayman enquiry. If his partner now bids no-trumps he was obviously searching for a spade fit, and opener can then bid spades if this is expedient.

If the opponents double the 1NT opening bid, most players agree that 2♣ is no longer Stayman, but is a weak take-out into clubs.

Play of suit contracts

As in the play of no-trump contracts, declarer must plan his play before touching a card in dummy. In suit contracts it is easiest to start by counting one's *losers*; then count the winners and make sure that the winners + losers add up to 13. This simple procedure will often help you to plan the play. On many hands you need only draw trumps and then play as you would in a no-trump contract, making extra tricks in suits having good intermediate cards, in long suits or by finesses, as already explained. Hold-up plays can still be useful but are less common than in no-trump contracts. In suit play extra tricks can also be made by using dummy's trumps to trump (to ruff) losers in declarer's hand. It is also possible, on some hands, to establish long suits without loss, because you can ruff the losers in the suit instead of giving them up as you would have to do in no-trumps.

♠ 10 9 8 7 5 4   *Deal 11.* Partner opens 1NT (15-17 points). What
♡ 4 3   do you respond?
◊ 6 5
♣ 10 6 4

Even if partner is maximum (17 points) he will have a terrible time playing in no-trumps with your hand as dummy. You, therefore, bid 2♠, a weak take-out in your long suit and partner *must* pass. If your partner had opened a weak no-trump you would have made the same weak take-out.

The bidding

	You	Partner
		1NT
	2♠	NB

Having bid his hand completely with the opening bid of 1NT, partner is correct to pass 2♠. He should not be tempted into bidding again even if you had bid hearts, a suit which his hand (see below) fits well.

North leads the ◊K against West's contract of 2♠. Plan the play.

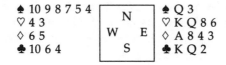

♠ 10 9 8 7 5 4   ♠ Q 3
♡ 4 3   ♡ K Q 8 6
◊ 6 5   ◊ A 8 4 3
♣ 10 6 4   ♣ K Q 2

Planning: Count the losers from declarer's point of view; three in spades, one in hearts, one in diamonds, and possibly two in clubs if South has the ♣A. Check by counting the winners, three in spades, one in hearts, one in diamonds and one in clubs. There are, therefore, seven losers and six winners, so it adds up. Is there any chance of making an extra trick? Yes, if North has the ♡A you can lead through him twice, so making both your ♡K and ♡Q. If this fails, you can try the same technique with clubs, so reducing your club losers to one. Entries to your own hand will be a problem but you should be able to get in by ruffing red suits.

The play: Win with the ◊A. Take every opportunity to draw trumps when in dummy but to finesse hearts (and later clubs) when in your own hand. So play a spade from dummy at trick 2. If the opponents win and continue diamonds, ruff the third round and lead a heart from your hand. If it wins, get off lead with a spade and repeat the heart finesse later; if it loses you will still have time to finesse clubs.

Postscript: Provided that either the heart or club finesse succeeds, and that trumps break normally, you should come to seven tricks. This is not a bad result as the opponents could have made at least a part-score. In no-trumps, partner would never be able to enter your hand, would have to lead away from his own high cards, and might well make only three tricks.

♠ A K 10 9 4   *Deal 12.* Partner opens 1NT (weak, 12-14 points).
♡ 7 6   What do you respond?
◊ K Q 4 2
♣ J 5

Even if partner is minimum (12 points rather than 14) there should be a fair chance of game on this hand. The only question is whether it should be played in 3NT or 4♠. You can leave the choice to partner by bidding 3♠, a forcing bid showing a strong hand with at least five spades. If partner has three spades he can raise to 4♠, knowing that you have at least eight trumps between you. If partner has a doubleton spade he should bid 3NT. He can't have less than two spades or his hand would not have been balanced enough for a no-trump opening bid.

The bidding   You   Partner
                               1NT
                       3♠   4♠

Having opened the bidding with 1NT, partner would not usually bid again but your jump response forces him to choose between 3NT or 4♠. With ♠Q-J-x (see below) he did not have a difficult choice.

North leads the ♡J against West's contract of 4♠. Plan the play.

♠ A K 10 9 4   ♠ Q J 8
♡ 7 6   N   ♡ Q 8 5
◊ K Q 4 2   W   E   ◊ J 10 9
♣ J 5   S   ♣ A K 9 7

Planning: North would not underlead the ♡A-K against a suit contract, so is likely to have led from a sequence (♡J-10-9) or possibly a doubleton. There are, therefore, two heart losers in addition to a diamond loser. The winners should be five spades, three diamonds (once the ◊A has been forced out) and two clubs.

The play: You can't do much about the hearts. If you play low from dummy, North will lead a second heart through. If you put up the ♡Q South will win with the ♡A or ♡K and continue the suit. You must trump (ruff) the third heart high (the ♠9 will do) to prevent the possibility of an over-ruff by North. Provided that trumps break normally you can now draw trumps and force out the ◊A to assure ten tricks for yourself.

Postscript: This is a simple hand if opponents' trumps are 3-2, but it can go sour if either defender fails to follow to the first or second round. A 5-0 split will defeat declarer but a 4-1 split can be dealt with by switching to diamonds the moment the bad trump break is revealed, so that the expected heart continuation can be ruffed in dummy, and declarer's trumps can be conserved.

♠ 8 5
♡ A Q J 7 3 2   *Deal 13.* Partner opens 1NT (weak, 12-14 points)
◊ Q 2   and your right hand opponent bids 2♠. What do
♣ A 8 6   you bid?

As in the last hand, this is a case of an opening bid opposite an opening bid, so a game contract should be reached. Here, however, you have a 6-card heart suit and you know partner must have at least two hearts in order to open 1NT. The obvious bid, therefore, is a direct 4♡, which must have a fair chance of success. The spades would be a danger in no-trumps even if the opponents had not bid the suit, and you would bid 4♡ whether or not the opponents intervened.

The bidding	*You*	*Partner*
		1NT (opponents overcall 2♠)
	4♡	

Having shown the type of hand that he holds with the opening bid of 1NT, partner must accept your decision as to the final contract even though his weakest suit is hearts.

North leads the ♣K and then ♣4 against West's contract of 4♡. South wins the second trick with the ♣10 and continues with the ♣A. Plan the play.

♠ 8 5   ┌─────────┐   ♠ Q 6 3
♡ A Q J 7 3 2   │   N   │   ♡ K 6
◊ Q 2   │ W   E │   ◊ A 9 5
♣ A 8 6   │   S   │   ♣ K J 5 3 2
                 └─────────┘

Planning: North's lead must surely be from a doubleton (♠K-x of his partner's suit). Count the possible losers from declarer's point of view; two in spades, none in hearts, one in diamonds, and one in clubs. Now count the winners; six in hearts, one in diamonds, and two in clubs. There are, therefore, nine winners and four losers. Next look for a way to convert at least one of the losers into a winner; obviously the long club suit can provide at least one extra trick and a losing diamond can be thrown on it.

The play: Ruff the third spade trick with the ♡J to prevent North from over-ruffing; draw trumps, low first to the ♡K so that you don't block the suit; play the ♣A and lead a low club to the ♣J. If this loses to the ♣Q there will only be one club left in the opponents' hands and this will fall to the ♣K on the next round. Declarer's losing diamond can be thrown on a winning club and the contract will be made for the loss of two spades and one club.

Postscript: If the club finesse succeeds and South discards, showing that North began with four clubs to the queen, cash the ♣K and ruff a club in your own hand to establish the suit. The ◊A provides an entry to the last club in dummy and you will make an overtrick.

Only if South holds the guarded ♣Q and the defence force out dummy's ◊A early, is the contract likely to fail.

♠ 6 2
♡ A 8 7 6
◊ A K 8
♣ Q J 4 3

Deal 14. You open 1NT (weak) and partner bids 2♣. What do you bid now?

2♣ is the Stayman convention. Partner is not showing a club suit but is exploring for a major suit contract and is asking you to bid a 4-card major suit if you have one or else to bid 2◊ (the conventional denial). On this hand you bid 2♡ and partner raises to 4♡.

The bidding	*You*	*Partner*
	1NT	2♣
	2♡	4♡

Partner's weakness in diamonds (see below) made him wish to explore for a possible suit contract, but he was prepared for any bid that you could make when he introduced Stayman. When the heart fit came to light, he was encouraged to bid game. If you had responded 2◊ or 2♠ he would have bid only 2NT, leaving it to you to bid 3NT on a maximum.

Players of the strong no-trump would have to open 1♣, planning to rebid 1NT. When partner responds 1♡, however, the correct rebid is 2♡, and partner will raise to 4♡. The same contract would be reached, therefore, but played by East.

North leads ♠J against West's contract of 4♡. South wins East's ♠K with the ♠A, cashes ♠Q and switches to a diamond. Plan the play.

$$
\begin{array}{c|c|c}
\begin{array}{l}
\spadesuit\ 6\ 2 \\
\heartsuit\ A\ 8\ 7\ 6 \\
\diamondsuit\ A\ K\ 8 \\
\clubsuit\ Q\ J\ 4\ 3
\end{array}
&
\begin{array}{c}
N \\
W \quad E \\
S
\end{array}
&
\begin{array}{l}
\spadesuit\ K\ 7\ 5 \\
\heartsuit\ K\ Q\ J\ 4 \\
\diamondsuit\ 7\ 5 \\
\clubsuit\ K\ 7\ 6\ 2
\end{array}
\end{array}
$$

Planning: Count the losers first. You have already lost two spades and might lose a diamond and a club. The diamond loser, however, can be ruffed in dummy. There is no indication as to how to play the clubs (it depends on who has the ♣A) but the best chance of making three club tricks is to lead low from one hand towards honour(s) in the opposite hand.

The play: Win the ◊A, draw trumps, cash ◊K and ruff a diamond in dummy. Lead a low club to the ♣J. Even if North wins with ♣A, a 3-2 club split will provide three club tricks for East-West.

Postscript: If the clubs behave, the contract should make with three club tricks, four trumps, two diamonds and a diamond ruff. Ruffing in dummy provides an extra trick; after a strong no-trump sequence, East's natural play for ten tricks (as declarer) would be to ruff a spade in the West hand (his dummy). The contract can make either way as there are four trumps in each hand. When tackling clubs it is a mistake to *lead* a club honour; if *either* opponent has the singleton ace, you will have found a foolproof way to lose two club tricks.

♠ Q 2   *Deal 15.* Partner opens 1NT (strong). What do you
♡ 6 3   respond?
◊ 6 5
♣ 10 9 8 6 5 4 2

Even if partner has a powerful hand, he is going to be in trouble in
1NT; he will never be able to get into your hand to make any clubs,
and will be forced to keep leading suits away from his own high
cards, so will make very few tricks. You would like to bid 2♣ as a
weak take-out but unfortunately partner will think that this is a
Stayman bid and will start showing his major suits. However, 1NT
will be a disaster and there is nothing else for it but to keep bidding
clubs until partner gets the message.

The bidding	*You*	*Partner*
		1NT
	2♣	2♡
	3♣	NB

Partner responded 2♡ to your 2♣ bid, believing it to be Stayman,
but he was right to pass your 3♣ bid as, by then, he realised that
you had a weak hand with a long club suit. You can't stop in 2♣
over 1NT if you play the Stayman convention but this is a very
small disadvantage. The price you pay for using a conventional
bid is that you can no longer use that bid naturally. However, it is
a price worth paying, because the weak hand with long clubs is
much rarer than hands on which you want to explore for a major
suit contract.

*North leads the ◇3 against West's contract of 3♣. How many tricks do
you expect East-West to make? How many tricks do you think they
would have made if East played the hand in 1NT?*

♠ Q 2		♠ K 9 7
♡ 6 3	N	♡ K Q 7 5
◇ 6 5	W E	◇ A Q 4 2
♣ 10 9 8 6 5 4 2	S	♣ Q 7

If East-West were very lucky the clubs would split 2-2 and North
would have the ◇K and the ♡A. East-West would, in that case, lose
only four top tricks. In contrast, if every finesse is wrong and the
clubs break 4-0, East-West would make only seven tricks. On
average they will make about eight tricks and so be 'one down'.

  In 1NT the only certain tricks are one spade, one heart and the
◇A. No club tricks will be made because of the shortage of entries

to the West hand. Four tricks, with luck, is about the maximum that could be made in a contract of 1NT.

With such a weak distributional hand it is better to play in a suit contract, even at the three-level, than in 1NT. One down or even two down, is a reasonable result for East-West as it prevents the opponents from making a contract of their own.

CHAPTER 4

Suit Bidding and Play

To value a balanced hand you merely count the high card points (4 for an ace, etc) but with an unbalanced hand you add on distributional points (DP) as well. From now on points means high card points plus distributional points (HCP + DP). There are several systems of assessing distributional points but probably the simplest, *if you are considering opening the bidding*, is to add one extra point for each card over four in the prospective trump suit. A hand of about 13 points (or a good 12) justifies an opening bid and this could be all high card points in a balanced hand, 12 high card points and a 5-card suit, 11 high card points and two 5-card suits, ten high card points and a 6-card suit, etc.

If partner has opened the bidding and *you are considering a response*, you value your hand differently; provided you have 4-card support for his trump suit you can add distributional points for *shortages* in side suits on the scale 3 for a void, 2 for a singleton and 1 for a doubleton. The minimum number of points needed for a reply is 6 if this can be made at the one-level, for example 1♣-1♠, but at least 8 if it has to be made at the 2-level (1♠-2♣).

Players vary slightly in what they regard as a biddable suit but it is reasonable to consider any 4-card suit to be biddable. To rebid a suit (to bid the same suit twice) you must have at least five cards in it; to bid a suit three times you must have at least six cards in it.

A player should always try to bid his long suits first ('length before strength') but probably the most important rule for the opening bidder is that *before bidding a suit he should prepare his rebid*.

This is because modern bidding systems are *approach forcing*, that is, if you open the bidding, then partner (with certain minimum requirements) *must* reply and, when he does, this forces you to bid again. If there were no way of stopping, every sequence would end up in 7NT, but bidding can be brought to an end by the use of *limit-bids*. In the Acol system all bids and rebids in no-trumps (except those described later on p.74) are limit-bids, and so are bids of partner's suit, or rebids of one's own suit. Limit-bids are never forcing, so can be passed by partner unless he judges that a further bid is indicated. The action he takes will depend on the strength of his own hand but he should pass if he has nothing to spare.

Targets for the bidding

With average luck, 23 points in the combined partnership hands should bring home a contract of 3 of a suit (or 2NT). If you judge that the partnership has much more than this, say 25 points, then try to bid a game; if less, then try to stop the bidding. If you can find an 8-card fit in a suit (you have four, partner has four; you have five, partner has three, etc), then play in that suit, if not then play in no-trumps. However, it is usually better to abandon an 8-card fit in a minor suit in favour of a no-trump contract, as game in no-trumps needs only nine tricks, instead of eleven tricks for 5♣ or 5◊.

The bidding sequence

The minimum required for an opening bid is 10-11 high card points with a 6-card suit but the bid of one of a suit can be made on up to 19 points. A simple response can be made on as few as 6 points or as many as 15 points. In any bidding sequence the opener should assume that his partner is minimum for his response and, when choosing a limit-bid, he should bid as high as he dares. This will reveal opener's strength to his partner, who can then select the final contract. For example, if your partner opens 1♡ you would assume that he had enough points to open and at least four hearts. Suppose you respond 1♠ and he next bids 2NT. Now you must revise your opinion of his hand. It must be balanced (he rebid in no-trumps), and it must contain 17-18 points because you have guaranteed only 6. Now you simply add your values to his; if, for example, your hand were reasonably balanced and you had 8 points, you would bid 3NT.

Play of suit contracts

As already explained, on many hands the right way to play a suit contract is to draw trumps and then to play as if it were a no-trump contract. There are, however, some hands on which declarer must not draw trumps too soon, for example if dummy's trumps guard a weakness in declarer's hand or if declarer needs to ruff a side suit in dummy to establish the suit or make extra tricks.

♠ K 7 3   *Deal 16.* Partner opens 1◊. What do you respond
♡ Q 7 5 3   on this hand?
◊ 8 4 2
♣ Q 6 3

With 7 high card points you must respond, as partner may have opened one of a suit with up to 19 points. Don't respond 1NT 'just to show you are weak'. It's better to show the 4-card major suit by bidding 1♡. This bid has the same minimum (6 points) as a response of 1NT and partner must assume that you are minimum when making his rebid.

Partner raises 1♡ to 2♡, showing at least 4-card support. The 2♡ bid is a limit-bid (all raises of partner's suit are limit-bids), showing that he is strong enough for 2♡ but not for 3♡ or 4♡. Limit-bids can be passed; if you were stronger you could continue but you have practically no undisclosed strength and there is no reason to go on bidding now.

The bidding	*You*	*Partner*
		1◊
	1♡	2♡
	NB	

Partner raised your hearts with 10-x-x-x (see over) because he knew you had eight hearts between you. If you had responded

1NT your partner would have either passed or rebid his diamonds. Neither contract is as good as 2♡, as we shall see.

North leads the ◊7 against West's contract of 2♡. Plan the play.

```
        ♠ K 7 3        ┌──────┐        ♠ J 2
        ♡ Q 7 5 3      │   N  │        ♡ 10 6 4 2
        ◊ 8 4 2        │ W  E │        ◊ A K Q 9 5
        ♣ Q 6 3        │   S  │        ♣ A 2
                       └──────┘
```

Planning: If trumps break 3-2 there will be a trump left in dummy to ruff a black suit loser. The winners will be one heart, five diamonds, the ♣A and a club or spade ruff.

The play: As declarer, your best plan is to draw trumps and run the diamond suit. Don't be frightened to do this because of the poor quality of your trump suit. You have to lose three trump tricks and you must draw trumps as early as possible. The diamond lead is a warning that the opponents may be able to ruff the suit; one ruff may not hurt you as the opponents will possibly then only make two heart tricks, but two diamond ruffs could be fatal.

Postscript: If the hand is played in diamonds or no-trumps, fewer tricks will be made because there is no opportunity to obtain a ruff in dummy for an extra trick.

♠ A 8 4   *Deal 17.* What is your opening bid on this hand
♡ A J 10 7 4   and what is your rebid if partner responds 2♣?
◊ 9 3
♣ K 8 3

You should open 1♡ and rebid 2♡, guaranteeing at least five cards in your suit. 2♡ is a limit-bid, not showing any great strength over and above that required to open. Your partner now jumps to 4♡.

The bidding	You	Partner
	1♡	2♣
	2♡	4♡

When you open 1♡ partner can't raise the hearts immediately as you may have only four and he is deterred from no-trumps by the weakness in spades. He, therefore, makes the waiting bid of 2♣, which forces you to bid again. When your rebid tells him that you have at least five hearts, he can raise you directly to game.

North leads the ♠K against West's contract of 4♡. Plan the play.

♠ A 8 4	**N**	♠ 7 6
♡ A J 10 7 4	**W E**	♡ K Q 3
◊ 9 3	**S**	◊ J 7 5 4
♣ K 8 3		♣ A Q 4 2

Planning: Potential losers from declarer's point of view are two spades and two diamonds. It would be possible to discard a losing spade on dummy's last (winning) club if the suit broke 3-3, but this distribution is unlikely (see Appendix). The best way to avoid two spade losers is to ruff one of them in dummy. You can't afford to draw trumps on this hand but must get the spade ruff in first. Now check by counting winners; there are three club winners, five heart winners and the ♠A, so just one spade ruff will give you your contract.

The play: Win with the ♠A and play another spade immediately. If the opponents now switch to trumps, win in your own hand and lead another spade, ruffing with the ♡K or ♡Q to prevent a possible over-ruff. Now cash the remaining high trump in dummy, return to hand via the ♣K, draw the remaining trumps and cash your other winners.

Postscript: Some pairs may bid (and make) 3NT with these cards, as there are nine top tricks. They might, if the clubs break, even make an overtrick. But they might lose the first five diamond tricks. 4♡ is a safer contract.

♠ A K 2   *Deal 18*. What is your opening bid on this hand
♡ J 3 2   and what is your rebid if partner responds in
◊ A K 10 8 5 3   hearts?
♣ 2

You have 15 high card points and can add 2 points for the length in diamonds. Obviously you will bid diamonds but are you strong enough to open 2◊? In Acol you would require eight playing tricks in your own hand for this bid. To count playing tricks, assume that your long suit is trumps and that the outstanding cards break reasonably. So you can assume that your partner has a doubleton diamond and that the remaining five cards split 3-2. You would, therefore, expect to make five diamond tricks and two spades. Seven playing tricks is not enough to open 2◊ but is just right to open 1◊ and rebid 3◊.

The bidding	*You*	*Partner*
	1◊	1♡
	3◊	5◊

Partner correctly responded 1♡ to your opening bid and when he learnt that you had a seven-trick hand with a strong diamond suit he raised you to game in diamonds. With a stop in the club suit he might have tried 3NT.

North leads the ♣A against West's contract of 5◊ and continues with the ♣K. Plan the play.

♠ A K 2		♠ Q 10 3
♡ J 3 2	N	♡ A Q 5 4
◊ A K 10 8 5 3	W E	◊ Q 9 2
♣ 2	S	♣ 6 4 3

Planning: You have already lost one club trick and will probably lose a heart even if North has the ♡K. You can't afford any more losers. It is also possible that you could lose a diamond. If the suit splits 2-2 or 3-1 there is no problem, but one of your opponents may have ◊J-x-x-x, in which case you will have to play the suit with care. It is a mistake to play the ◊Q on the first round because you will lose a trick to North later if South has none.

The play: Ruff the ♣K and cash the ◊A. If South has none, lead a small diamond towards dummy and win with the ◊9 if North plays low. If North has no diamonds, go up with the ◊Q in dummy and lead the ◊9 through South next time.

Postscript: It's easy to become careless on hands that look simple. A little care in the play of the diamond suit will bring home the contract in spite of the awkward split.

♠ A 8 6 5   *Deal 19*. What is your opening bid on this hand?
♡ A K 10 2
◇ A 6 4 2
♣ 6

Ideas about the bidding of hands with 4-4-4-1 shape have changed in recent years, making it rare for a player to open with a major suit and rebid in another suit unless he has at least five cards in the major. The modern style is, (a) with a red singleton, open 1♣, (b) with a black singleton, open the middle suit. For example:

♠ x   ♠ A J x x
♡ A J x x   Middle ———→ ♡ A J x x
◇ A J x x ←——— suit   ◇ A J x x
♣ A J x x   ♣ x

Thus, on Deal 19, with a singleton ♣, the recommended opening bid is 1♡.

Partner responds 3♡. In Acol this is a limit-bid showing at least 4-card heart support and 10-12 points. You could pass this if you were minimum but, as you have 15 points, you know that there is enough for game, so you raise to 4♡.

The bidding	You	Partner
	1♡	3♡
	4♡	

Partner has only 8 high card points but, with such good trump support, he can add 2 points for the singleton spade, giving him enough for the double raise. The spade shortage will be very useful in the play, as we shall see.

North leads the ♡6 against West's contract of 4♡. Plan the play.

	N	
♠ A 8 6 5		♠ 4
♡ A K 10 7	W E	♡ Q J 4 3
◇ A 6 4 2		◇ J 8 7 5
♣ 6	S	♣ A 9 5 2

Planning: Count the possible losers from declarer's point of view; three in spades, and three in diamonds. The best chance lies in ruffing the three losing spades in dummy. The winners will then be the ♠A and three spade ruffs, two minor suit aces and four trumps. You will need four entries to your own hand to keep leading spades; the ♠A, the ◊A and two club ruffs will provide these. You will, therefore, play the hand as a classic 'cross-ruff', ruffing spades in dummy and clubs in your own hand, so making your trumps separately. Before embarking on the cross-ruff, cash your side suit winners early. This is to prevent an opponent from discarding minor suits, for example when you are ruffing spades, and then being able to trump your aces later.

The play: Do *not* draw trumps. Win the trump lead in your hand. Cash the ♠A and ruff a spade low; cash the ♣A, enter your hand with the ◊A, ruff the third spade with the ♡J, ruff a club, and ruff the last spade with the ♡Q. Now you will be left with the ♡A-K and three losing diamonds.

Postscript: Note that ruffing clubs in your own hand does not give extra tricks – you have already counted your four hearts as winners anyway. The club ruffs merely provide entries to your hand so that you can lead spades and ruff in dummy, which *does* provide three extra tricks.

CHAPTER 5
Distributional Hands

Showing the shape of the hand

Opener and responder should try to show the shape of their hands by bidding their long suits first ('length before strength'). However, they must remember the targets for the bidding (p.41) and not go beyond the level of contract they can make. Some general guidelines follow.

Six-card suits

Provided the bidding does not get too high:

1 A good-quality 6-card suit can be bid three times.
2 With a 6-card suit and a 5-card suit (a 6-5 shape) open the 6-card suit, then bid and rebid the 5-card suit.
3 With 6-4 shape, generally bid the 6-card suit twice and then bid the 4-card suit. However, with a 6-card minor and a 4-card major you may be able to open the minor and show the major at the one-level, for example 1♣-1♡, 1♠- etc, and repeat the minor suit later.

Five-card suits

Provided the bidding does not get too high:

1 A good-quality 5-card suit can be bid and rebid.

2 With 5-5 shape, generally bid the higher-ranking suit first, then bid and rebid the lower-ranking suit. With the two black suits, however, the bidding is kept lower if clubs are bid first.

3 With 5-4 shape bid the 5-card suit and then either rebid the 5-card suit or bid the 4-card suit (see below).

Keeping the bidding low

Consider the bidding of the following hand:

♠ J 6
♡ K Q 10 8 5
◊ A J 4 3
♣ K 6

There is no problem in showing both suits. You open 1♡ and, if partner responds 1♠, 1NT or 2♣, you can bid 2◊, giving him a choice betweeen your two suits at the two-level.

If, however, the spades and diamonds were exchanged, there would be a problem. If you open 1♡ and partner responds 1NT or 2♣, you can't now show your spades; if he doesn't like your second suit he may have to put you back to your first suit and you will have arrived in 3♡ when you have only 14 high card points and he may have only 6 (if he bid 1NT) or 8 (if he bid 2♣).

In the sequence 1♡-1NT-2♠ opener has 'reversed'. A reverse occurs when opener bids two suits in such an order that his partner cannot give preference to the first suit below the three-level. A reverse often occurs when opener bids a lower-ranking suit before a higher-ranking suit, as in the example above, but it is not confined to this situation. For example 1♠-2♡-3♣ is a reverse (known as a 'high reverse') and so is 1♡-2◊-3♣ because opener could have kept the bidding lower if he had bid his suits the other way round.

To reverse, opener must know that there are at least 23 points in the combined hands. Thus, if responder has shown 6, opener must have at least 17. A reverse guarantees a longer first than second suit (at least 5-4 shape) to justify this expensive way of bidding.

The reverse bid is generally regarded as forcing for one round, particularly when made over a two-level response.

Four-card suits

Hands with two 4-card suits can be difficult to bid. With the two black suits the correct opening is 1♣ with a 1♠ rebid; however, with a different combination of 4-card suits, the experts differ in their views.

Many of the hands with 4-4-3-2 shape are best opened 1NT, if the point count is suitable, or opened with one of the four-card suits and rebid in no-trumps. The latter course of action raises the question of which suit to open and which to ignore. Although there appears to be no perfect answer, the style of bidding a major suit in preference to a minor suit has many adherents. It prevents the partnership missing a major suit fit and is more pre-emptive than a minor suit opening, although on some hands a minor suit fit will be missed.

Fourth suit forcing

If partner has opened in one suit, you have responded in another and he has made his rebid in a third suit, there will seldom be much point in bidding the fourth suit genuinely; partner has shown at least eight cards in *his* suits and is unlikely to be able to support your second suit. For example, if partner opens 1♡ and you respond 1♠ on

  ♠ K Q 5 4
  ♡ J 5
  ◇ K J 8 2
  ♣ Q 8 3

and partner's rebid is 2♣, your natural bid is now 2NT, not 2◇. Therefore, as you are unlikely to want to bid the fourth suit naturally you can, by agreement, use the bid conventionally to ask partner to describe his hand further. For example, if you hold

  ♠ K Q 7 6 5
  ♡ K 6 5
  ◇ Q 9
  ♣ K 7 2

and the bidding goes 1♡ from partner, 1♠ from you, 2♣ from partner, you can now bid 2◇ (fourth suit forcing) showing no particular holding in the diamond suit but forcing partner to bid again, to describe his hand further. He can bid his hearts again (showing at least five), give delayed support for spades (showing three) or bid no-trumps if he has a guard in diamonds. Whichever he does, you will have found the right denomination in which to play the contract, and you can raise to the appropriate level.

♠ A 9 3 2   *Deal 20.* What is your opening bid on this hand
♡ A K Q 5 2   and what is your rebid if partner bids diamonds?
◊ J 6
♣ Q 2

The rule is 'bid your longest suit first' so you must open 1♡. When partner responds 2◊ he guarantees at least 8 points and you know that you have at least 24 points between you; you can, therefore, 'reverse' into 2♠ to explore for a possible spade fit, knowing that, if partner does not like your second suit, he can bid 3◊ or 3♡, and you will still not be out of your depth. You have made a *reverse bid*, showing a strong hand with the first bid suit longer than the second. With a weaker hand you would have to rebid your hearts because you would not be strong enough to risk a three-level contract.

Over 2♠ partner jumps to 4♡ and you pass.

The bidding	You	Partner
	1♡	2◊
	2♠	4♡

Partner realised that you must have at least 15 points because you were prepared to play at the three-level even though his first response guaranteed only 8 points. He also realised that you had more hearts than spades because with 5-5 shape you would have bid the higher-ranking suit first. With 3-card support for hearts and 10 points he was strong enough to go to game.

North leads the ♣Q against West's contract of 4♡ and South encourages with the ♣7. Plan the play.

♠ A 9 3 2		♠ 8 5
♡ A K Q 5 2	N	♡ J 8 3
◊ J 6	W E	◊ K Q 10 9 4
♣ Q 2	S	♣ A 4 3

Planning: The potential losers are three spades, one diamond and one club. However, the diamonds will provide three discards, so the contract can be made (with an overtrick) with one spade winner, five hearts, four diamonds and one club. But there is one big danger; if you win with the ♠A, draw trumps and force out the ♢A, the opponents will then be able to cash three spade tricks. Dummy's trumps protect your spade weakness so you can't afford to let the opponents in after dummy's trumps are gone. The solution is to set up the diamonds before drawing trumps.

The play: Duck the first spade to break communications between opponents' hands. Win the second spade with the ♠A. Play on diamonds until the ♢A is forced out. The worst that can happen is that the opponents will make the ♢A and a diamond ruff. You can then win any return, draw trumps and you should have ten tricks.

Postscript: Counting winners only would suggest that there are eleven tricks for the taking but a count of the losers pinpoints the spade weakness and suggests the right line of play.

♠ A 3	*Deal 21*. What opening bid would you make on
♡ A K 10 2	this hand, and what is your rebid if partner bids
♢ K J 10 8 4	spades?
♣ Q 3	

This is a good hand, with 17 high card points plus an extra for the fifth diamond, so is well up to strength for planning a 'reversing' sequence. If partner can bid at all, there is a good chance for game. You open 1♢ and, when partner responds 1♠, reverse into 2♡. This, you will remember, is forcing, and partner is expected to rebid in the most sensible way he can. With a good stop in clubs he would rebid in no-trumps at the appropriate level. In fact he raises your hearts to 3♡ and you, with a now guaranteed 4-4 heart fit, bid the game.

The bidding	You	Partner
	1♢	1♠
	2♡	3♡
	4♡	

With a 6-card spade suit, 1♠ was partner's obvious response.

When forced by your rebid to respond again, even on only 6 high card points, he clearly has no interest in no-trumps but is happy to agree your second suit. The partnership has eight cards in each major suit, but the contract will play better in the 4-4 fit than in the 6-2 fit, as the play will show.

North leads the ♡6 against West's contract of 4♡. Plan the play.

♠ A 3
♡ A K 10 2
◇ K J 10 8 4
♣ Q 3

♠ K 9 7 5 4 2
♡ Q J 9 4
◇ 3
♣ 4 2

Planning: West appears to have a disconcerting number of minor suit losers, but a 3-2 spade break will enable declarer to establish the suit without loss for three discards. To establish spades without losing a trick, which clearly you can't afford, it will be necessary to trump a spade in the West hand. In this case, dummy's trumps will have to be used to draw the opponents' trumps, a procedure known as a 'dummy reversal', for which you will need to have good high trumps in dummy. These you have, and the winners, if all goes well, will be five spades, one spade ruff in the West hand, and four hearts.

The play: Win the first trick in the West hand with a high trump, saving dummy's high trumps for the 'reversal'. Cash the ♠A and cross to the ♠K, hoping that both opponents will follow. Ruff a third spade high, to prevent North from over-ruffing. Play off the remaining high trump in the West hand, cross to dummy with the ♡2, draw any outstanding trumps, and run the established spades.

Postscript: The contract will make as long as neither opponent has a singleton or void in spades, even if the trumps break 4-1. If played in spades, at least one spade trick will be lost in addition to three tricks in the minors, once again proving that the 4-4 fit is the superior spot to play the hand.

♠ K Q 9 8 5   *Deal 22. What is your opening bid on this hand?*
♡ 6 5
◇ A Q 8 7 5 3
♣ –

Although you have only 11 high card points, the playing strength of the two good suits makes this a respectable hand. You open your long suit first, with a bid of 1◊ and hope to be able to bid the spades twice to show the 6-5 shape. Over 1◊ your partner bids 1♡ so you bid 1♠ as planned. Partner now bids 2♣ (fourth suit forcing) and you complete the picture with a bid of 2♠. Partner now raises you to 4♠ and you pass.

The bidding	*You*	*Partner*
	1◊	1♡
	1♠	2♣
	2♠	4♠

In fact, partner had a genuine club suit (see below) but this wasn't guaranteed when he bid it as the fourth suit, to gain more information about your hand. When he learnt that you had a rebiddable spade suit he was able to raise direct to game.

North leads the ♣J against West's contract of 4♠. Dummy's ♣Q is played and South plays the ♣A. Plan the play.

```
    ♠ K Q 9 8 5                ♠ A 10 3
    ♡ 6 5          N           ♡ K 8 7 3 2
    ◊ A Q 8 7 5 3  W     E     ◊ K
    ♣ —               S        ♣ K Q 3 2
```

Planning: To establish the diamonds you will probably need to ruff in dummy. The ◊K blocks the suit and you will have to find a way back to your hand before you can get a diamond ruff.

The play: Refuse to shorten your trumps by ruffing the ♣A. Discard a heart instead. The best that South can now do is to cash his ♡A, before you can discard your second heart on the ♣K and, because a spade lead would help you find the ♠J, to exit with another heart. Declarer plays dummy's ◊K, returns to his hand with a club ruff, ruffs a low diamond with dummy's ♠10, plays ♠A and another to the ♠K-Q. If an opponent has the ♠J left (a 4-1 split) declarer can run the diamonds to force it out and can trump in with his last spade later.

Postscript: Declarer should be careful not to shorten his trumps prematurely. He will need to ruff a club to lead a diamond for dummy to trump. If he has shortened his trumps already he will be down to three and will lose control of the hand if trumps split badly.

♠ A 8 7 3 2   *Deal 23.* How do you plan the bidding of this
♡ A K J 7 2   hand?
◇ 7
♣ Q 6

Fourteen high card points plus good distributional values makes quite a powerful hand. Although the hearts are stronger than the spades, the rule with two 5-card suits is to bid the higher-ranking suit first and then to bid the lower-ranking suit twice, provided that this does not take the bidding too high.

The bidding	*You*	*Partner*
	1♠	**2♣**
	2♡	**3◇**
	3♡	**4♡**

Partner's first response showed a minimum of 8 points. His second bid was fourth suit forcing, asking you to describe your hand more fully, which you did by rebidding your second suit. When he learns that you have rebiddable hearts, his own 3-card support (see below) is sufficient to agree the suit.

North cashes the ◇A and then leads the ♠J against West's contract of 4♡. Dummy's ♠Q is covered by South's ♠K. Plan the play.

♠ A 8 7 5 3		♠ Q 6
♡ A K J 7 2	N	♡ Q 4 3
◇ 7	W E	◇ Q 10 2
♣ Q 6	S	♣ A K 9 3 2

Planning: The spades have gone badly so there are, potentially, four spade and one diamond losers. However, one spade can be thrown on a club and another can be ruffed in dummy. The winners should then be the ♠A and a spade ruff, five hearts and three clubs.

The play: Win the second trick with the ♠A and lead another spade immediately. When you regain the lead, continue with a third spade and ruff high in dummy. Draw trumps and cash the club winners.

Postscript: The suggested line of play requires a 3-2 trump split and spades no worse than 4-2. An alternative line is to set up the clubs for discards. To do this, you would lead the ♣Q at trick three, then a low club to the ♣A. You would not cash the ♣K but would lead a *low* club from dummy and ruff high in your own hand. You would then draw three rounds of trumps, ending in dummy and play ♣K and another, discarding two losers from your own hand.

♠ A J 3 2　　　　*Deal 24.* What is your opening bid on this hand?
♡ K J 4 2
◊ Q
♣ K 6 4 2

This hand is not worth its 14 high card points because the singleton ◊Q is most unlikely to make a trick. However, it's too strong to be passed. With 4-4-4-1 shape containing a singleton diamond it is best to open 1♣ to give yourself the best chance of finding a suit fit; if partner responds 1♡ or 1♠ you can raise his suit, but if he responds 1◊, you can continue to explore with a bid of 1♡.

The bidding	*You*	*Partner*
	1♣	1◊
	1♡	4♡

Although partner has six diamonds (see below) he is right to abandon them in favour of the heart suit when he learns from your rebid that you have four hearts. The 4-4 major suit fit provides a much better chance of game than the minor suit, and the diamonds will take tricks in either contract.

North leads the ◊8 against West's contract of 4♡. Plan the play.

♠ A J 3 2　　　　　　　♠ —
♡ K J 4 2　　　N　　　♡ A Q 9 3
◊ Q　　　W　　E　　◊ A J 10 9 7 3
♣ K 6 4 2　　　S　　　♣ 9 7 3

Planning: That lead is very unlikely to be 'low from an honour', that is, away from the ◊K, and may well be a singleton or doubleton. If you allow South to win, he may return the ♣Q through your ♣K and you may lose one diamond and three club tricks straightaway. There are two possible ways of playing the hand. You can either lead spades from your own hand, ruff in dummy and lead diamonds from dummy to ruff in your own hand (a 'cross-ruff') or else you can plan to set up the diamond suit and to discard your losers on it. The second plan is preferable because of the danger of being over-ruffed by North.

The play: Go up with the ◊A and draw three rounds of trumps, ending in dummy. Lead the ◊J; if South plays the ◊K, ruff it, play the ♠A and then ruff a spade to gain entry to dummy's remaining diamonds; if South plays low on the ◊J discard a black loser and continue to lead diamonds and discard black losers until the ◊K is forced out.

Postscript: The play of the ◊J through South's ◊K to your void is known as a 'ruffing finesse'. Even if the opponents were fooling you and North has the ◊K after all, the contract will be safe, for if North wins the lead with the ◊K he won't be able to attack clubs without giving you a club trick.

♠ K J 3
♡ A K 9 6 2   *Deal 25.* Partner opens the bidding with 1◊. You
◊ 5 4   respond 1♡ and his rebid is 1♠. What do you bid
♣ J 9 7   now?

This is a case of an opening bid opposite an opening bid, so a game contract should be possible if you can find a fit. What exactly has partner got? At least four diamonds (or five) and at least four spades. You don't know at this point how his other cards are distributed. What about his strength? Although he has bid his lower-ranking suit before his higher-ranking suit, he has not reversed, which he would have done if the bidding had gone 1♠-2♡-3◊ – etc. He has, therefore, bid his suits in the order which keeps the bidding low, so he has not guaranteed any more than bare opening strength.

    You need to find out more about the hand and the best way to do this is to bid 2♣ ('fourth suit forcing') to see if he can repeat his spades, support your hearts or bid no-trumps if he has a club stop. Over 2♣ he bids 2♡, showing 3-card support (with 4-card support he would have raised your hearts immediately) and you are strong enough to bid 4♡.

The bidding	*You*	*Partner*
		1◊
	1♡	1♠
	2♣	2♡
	4♡	

Partner opened his long suit first (see below) and was able to show his spades over 1♡. If you had responded 1NT or 2♣ he would have had to rebid 2◊. After your 'fourth suit forcing' bid he was right to show delayed support for hearts, having three.

North leads the ♡8 against West's contract of 4♡. Plan the play.

♠ K J 3	N	♠ A 8 5 2
♡ A K 9 6 2	W E	♡ Q 7 4
◊ 5 4	S	◊ K Q J 10 7
♣ J 9 7		♣ 4

Planning: The potential losers are one spade, one diamond and three clubs. Without the trump lead you might have been able to ruff two losing clubs in dummy, but that is hopeless now because the opponents will lead another trump when they win the first club trick. The obvious line of play is to set up dummy's diamonds and throw club losers on them. However, if you draw trumps and lead a diamond, the opponents will win and then cash three clubs, so you must save dummy's trumps until after the diamonds have been established.

The play: Win the lead in your own hand and lead a diamond towards the ◊K. If this wins, continue with the ◊Q. The worst that can happen is that South will win and lead a third diamond for his partner to ruff. If this happens, discard a club from your own hand – don't risk being over-ruffed by North. You will still make three diamond tricks, five hearts and two spades.

Postscript: The trap on this hand is to draw trumps before playing on diamonds. When dummy's trumps are the only protection for a weakness in your own hand, you have to establish the long suit first. We had a similar hand before (Deal 20).

CHAPTER 6

Special Bidding Sequences

The jump shift

The jump in a new suit, known as a *jump shift* or a *forcing take-out*, is a method of making sure that partner keeps the bidding open until game, at least, is reached.

A jump shift by responder, such as 1♡-2♠ or 1♡-3♣ shows a hand on which game is certain and a slam possible. The usual strength is 16 or more points but much depends on how well the hands fit and whether there is a strong suit that will take many tricks.

A jump shift by opener (1♡-1♠-3♣- etc or 1♡-2♣-3♢- etc) shows a hand that will guarantee game even if partner is minimum for his reply, that is about 19 points in the first sequence, and at least 17 points in the second sequence.

It will help the bidding sequence if, over partner's jump shift, you make the bid that you were planning to make before but, of course, at one level higher; it's partner who has raised the level, not you. For example, if you open 1♢, intending to bid 1♠ over 1♡, but your partner responds 2♡, you should now bid 2♠. Similarly in the sequence 1♣-2♢-2NT- etc opener is showing a hand that would have opened 1♣ and rebid 1NT over 1♢.

A jump bid in response to a forcing two bid has a special meaning; it shows a completely solid, self-supporting suit (six cards to the top four honours or seven cards to the A-K-Q).

Trial bids and cue-bids

Trial bids are usually made when a major suit has been opened and raised. For example, in the sequence 1♠-2♠-3♣, the bid of 3♣ is a trial bid. It is *not* an attempt to find a club fit (the partnership has already agreed spades). The message is that opener is strong enough to explore for a possible game in spades but not strong enough to bid it by himself; he needs help in the club suit. If responder is maximum for his 2♠ reply he should bid 4♠. If he is minimum he should sign off in 3♠. If he is intermediate, say 7-8 points, he should bid 4♠ if he can help in the club suit (eg, if he has high cards in clubs or if he is short of clubs and can trump) but bid 3♠ if his clubs are poor (eg ♣ x-x-x).

In contrast, if the bidding goes 1♠-3♠-4♣, the 4♣ bid commits the partnership to game and so is not a trial bid but a cue-bid. The message is that opener can guarantee game and is interested in a slam; he has first round control of the club suit. Cue-bid sequences are dealt with in more detail on p.75.

Playing the odds

One is often faced with the situation of having eight or nine cards of a suit in the combined hands but missing the queen. The books say that with eight cards you should finesse for the queen ('eight ever'), and with nine cards you should not finesse ('nine never'), but play out the A and K hoping the queen will drop. The first part of the rule is sound but with nine cards the odds of playing for the drop or finessing are very close. Nevertheless, it is better to be consistent and stick to one line of play unless there are specific reasons for not doing so. A little publicised but great advantage of following the 'nine never' rule is that, even if the queen doesn't drop, declarer retains the lead and can dictate the next move.

♠ A J 8 7 2   *Deal 26.* Your opening bid of 1♠ is raised to 2♠ by
♡ A K 3   your partner. What do you bid now?
◇ 7
♣ A 10 9 3

If partner is maximum for his raise (9 points) there may be a game contract. Much would depend on whether he can help you in clubs; if his strength is mainly in diamonds the hands won't fit well and game won't be possible.

Bid 3♣, a trial bid, showing that you are worth 3♠ but that a 4♠ contract will depend on partner being maximum, or being at least intermediate in strength with a good fit in clubs. Partner can sign off in 3♠ if he is weak or if your club bid doesn't suit his hand.

The bidding	*You*	*Partner*
	1♠	2♠
	3♣	4♠

Partner recognised 3♣ as a trial bid, not necessarily showing a biddable 4-card suit but showing the suit in which you most needed help. With good support for clubs (see below) his 8-point hand was enough to raise you to game.

North leads the ♡2 against West's contract of 4♠. Plan the play.

```
♠ A J 8 7 2         ┌─────┐        ♠ K 6 5 4
♡ A K 3             │  N  │        ♡ 6 5 4
◇ 7              W  │     │  E     ◇ Q 8 5
♣ A 10 9 3          │  S  │        ♣ Q J 7
                    └─────┘
```

Planning: There is one potential loser in each suit. However, one of dummy's hearts can be thrown on a club and a heart can be ruffed in dummy later to make one extra trick. You should then make at least four spade tricks, two hearts, a heart ruff and at least three clubs. With nine trumps, missing the queen, there is little to choose between playing for the drop or finessing. On this deal it is convenient to play for the drop (the ♠A then the ♠K) so that you are in the right hand to take the club finesse.

The play: Win the lead with the ♡A. Play the ♠A and a low spade to dummy's ♠K. If the ♠Q doesn't drop, abandon trumps and play the ♣Q from dummy, finessing South for the ♣K. Even if the ♣Q loses to the ♣K in the North hand, the clubs will be established. Declarer should be able to discard one of dummy's hearts on a club and to ruff a heart in dummy for his tenth trick. A defender who has the ♠Q left and is able to ruff with it will not necessarily defeat the contract as he will have given up his natural trump trick.

Postscript: Having failed to find the ♠Q, the way to go down in this contract is to play a third spade to draw the queen. The opponents will then force out your other top heart and, if the club finesse fails, they will cash a third heart before you can discard one from dummy.

♠ J 4 2   *Deal 27.* Partner raises your opening bid of 1♡ to
♡ A K 10 4 2   4♡. What do you bid now?
◊ 7 3
♣ A K 10

In the old days, partner's direct raises of your suit were simple affairs. With less than 6 points he would pass, with 6-9 points and at least 4-card trump support he would raise to the 2-level, with 10-12 points and trump support he would raise to the 3-level, and with 13-15 points and trump support he would raise to the 4-level. Nowadays, the first three responses remain the same but hands of game-going strength are bid by means of the delayed game raise (p.64) and the immediate raise to game, such as 1♡-4♡, is made on hands that have good trump support but are weak in the other suits, to pre-empt the opponents out of a contract of their own.

There is, therefore, no temptation to bid on and you should pass.

The bidding   *You*   *Partner*
                     1♡   4♡
                     NB

Partner's hand is really weak but with excellent trump support (see below). Undoubtedly he has prevented the opponents from reaching a good spade or diamond contract.

North leads the ◊Q against West's contract of 4♡. After taking the first two diamond tricks, the defenders cash the ♠A and lead another spade. Plan the play.

```
        ♠ J 4 2           ┌───────┐      ♠ 6
        ♡ A K 10 4 2      │   N   │      ♡ Q J 8 6 5
        ◊ 7 3             │ W   E │      ◊ K 2
        ♣ A K 10          │   S   │      ♣ J 9 7 5 3
                          └───────┘
```

Planning: Having lost three tricks already it is essential not to lose any more. There are no heart losers but the question is how to play the clubs. With only eight clubs in the combined hands you will have to finesse for the ♣Q.

The play: Ruff the second spade in dummy and draw trumps in two or three rounds. Play the ♣A. If the ♣Q does not drop, enter dummy with a spade ruff and lead a low club, finessing the ♣10 if South does not play the ♣Q.

Postscript: This play of the club suit gives the best chance of success but will fail if North has the queen and at least one other club. By playing the ♣A before taking the club finesse, declarer ensures that he does not lose to a singleton ♣Q with North.

♠ K J 10 9 8   *Deal 28*. You open 1♠ and your partner responds
♡ Q 10 5 4   2♣. What is your rebid?
◇ K 3
♣ A 3

The correct rebid is 2♡, not 2♠. Some players think that to show a new suit at the 2-level indicates a stronger hand than the simple rebid of the first suit. This is not true if opener's second suit is lower-ranking than his first. To put it another way, if 2♠ is regarded as a weak rebid, then 2♡, a lower bid, should not be regarded as showing extra strenth. The advantage of bidding 2♡ is obvious. Responder could have five clubs and four hearts and if opener doesn't show the suit, a heart fit could be missed.

Over 2♡ partner bids 4♠. What sort of hand does he hold?

A hand of at least opening bid strength and good spade support. His 2♣ may or may not show a genuine biddable suit as he has made a delayed game raise.

The bidding	*You*	*Partner*
	1♠	2♣
	2♡	4♠

Partner's jump to game on the second round is based on a stronger hand (see below) than he would have needed for a direct pre-emptive raise of 1♠ to 4♠. His 2♣ waiting bid was, in fact, based on a genuinely biddable suit but he might have had to bid a 3-card suit if his shape had been 4-3-3-3. For example, with:

♠ A 6 5 4
♡ K J 3
◇ J 6 2
♣ K Q 6

he would have been forced to bid in the same way.

North leads the ♡9 against West's contract of 4♠. South wins with the ♡A and returns a heart, North following with the ♡2. Plan the play.

```
            ♠ K J 10 9 8    ┌─────────┐   ♠ A 6 5 4
            ♡ Q 10 5 4      │    N    │   ♡ K J 3
            ◇ K 3           │ W     E │   ◇ J 2
            ♣ A 3           │    S    │   ♣ K J 6 2
                            └─────────┘
```

Planning: That heart lead is almost certainly from a doubleton and North is hoping to get a heart ruff. You must, therefore, get the trumps out quickly. The potential losers from West's point of view are one spade, one heart and two diamonds. However, one of dummy's diamonds can be thrown on a heart, and a diamond ruffed in dummy later.

The play: Win the second heart trick in dummy with the ♡K to unblock the suit. Take two top spade tricks. If South discards on the second spade, you can throw North in with the ♣Q as he can't attack diamonds without giving you a diamond trick. If South still has the ♣Q you must not let him in to lead a diamond, so your best chance is to play on hearts, overtaking the ♡J with the ♡Q and then leading the ♡10 and discarding a diamond from dummy.

Postscript: The defence helped you. South could have held up his ♡A so that your heart suit was not so easily established or he could have played back a diamond, putting you to an awkward guess.

As declarer you should never play on the assumption that the defence will be bad but it does no harm to give the defenders the chance to go wrong and to take advantage of any error they make.

♠ A K 10
♡ Q J 4
◇ Q 10 5 3
♣ K J 2

Deal 29. Playing the weak no-trump (12-14 points), you open 1◇ and partner responds 2♡. What is your rebid?

If partner had responded 1♡ you would have rebid 1NT. Now that he has responded 2♡, you should bid 2NT. You should make your planned rebid but, of course, at one level higher. Avoid the mistake of going straight to game because you know partner is strong; the sequence 1◊-2♡-3NT shows a hand that would have bid 2NT over a response of 1♡. If you go straight to 3NT, announcing values you have not got, it will be your fault if partner plunges on for a slam on insufficient values.

The bidding	You	*Partner*
	1◊	2♡
	2NT	4NT
	6NT	

Partner has 17 points (see below) and must make a jump shift. Your rebid shows a balanced hand of 15-16 points and he can now bid 4NT, a quantitative bid, requesting you to bid 6NT if you are maximum.

North leads the ♡3 against West's contract of 6NT. Plan the play.

```
      ♠ A K 10        ┌─────┐    ♠ J 4
      ♡ Q J 4         │  N  │    ♡ A K 7 2
      ◊ Q 10 5 3    W │     │ E  ◊ A K 4
      ♣ K J 2         │  S  │    ♣ Q 8 7 3
                      └─────┘
```

Planning: The certain winners are two spades, four hearts, three diamonds and two clubs (once the ♣A has been forced out). One more trick is needed somewhere. Possible sources of an extra trick are to find the doubleton ♣A or the ♠Q with South, or a 3-3 split in clubs or diamonds. You must make the most of all these chances.

The play: Win with the ♡J or ♡Q, lead a diamond to dummy's ◊A or ◊K and return a low club to the ♣J. If this wins, enter dummy with another diamond and lead a second low club towards the ♣K. If South now plays the ♣A you have three club tricks. If, on the other hand, North wins with the ♣A and leads a heart, win in the West hand and play off the ♠A, unblocking with ♠J to retain a finessing position against South. Now try the club split and the diamond split and, if both fail, return to dummy's winning hearts before finessing spades.

Postscript: The suggested line of play has a very high probability of success. Also, the opponents may have trouble with their discards. Although squeeze technique is outside the scope of this book, it is worth noting that, by the time you are down to the last three cards (as shown in the diagram below)

♠ K 10		♠ 4
♡ –	N	♡ K
◊ 10	W E	◊ –
♣ –	S	♣ 8

and dummy's ♡K is played, neither opponent will be able to retain the guarded ♠Q as well as a minor suit winner, so the discards will be well worth watching.

♠ A K Q J 9 7   *Deal 30.* Partner opens 2♡, a strong bid showing at
♡ 5 4 2   least eight playing tricks if hearts are trumps.
◊ 8 3   What do you respond?
♣ 6 4

The 2♡ opening bid is forcing for one round, so even with no points you would have to make a reply. Here you have an absolutely solid suit of your own and you can show this by a jump bid in a forcing situation. So you bid 3♠, showing a solid suit such as A-K-Q-J-x-x or A-K-Q-x-x-x-x and your partner raises you to 7♠.

The bidding

	You	Partner
		2♡
	3♠	7♠

Let's face it, partner has certainly pushed the boat out. His hand (see below) was somewhat substandard for an Acol two bid and his leap to 7♠ was wildly over-enthusiastic. These things do happen, however, and having been landed in the grand slam it is up to West to try and make the best of it.

North leads the ♣A against West's contract of 7♠. Plan the play.

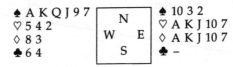

♠ A K Q J 9 7		♠ 10 3 2
♡ 5 4 2	N	♡ A K J 10 7
◊ 8 3	W E	◊ A K J 10 7
♣ 6 4	S	♣ –

Planning: There is no trump or diamond loser and the clubs can be ruffed in dummy but the problem is the possible losing heart. You could finesse against the ♡Q, but it's better to set up the diamond suit for discards.

The play: Ruff the ♣A with the ♠2. Play off the ◊A-K and ruff a third diamond high. If the ◊Q doesn't fall, enter dummy by ruffing a club with the ♠10, lead another diamond and ruff high again. By now the ◊Q should have fallen. Draw trumps, enter dummy with a heart and throw a heart on the established diamond.

Postscript: The contract should make if the diamonds are no worse than 4-2, a much better prospect than a finesse.

CHAPTER 7

Strong Hands

Valuing strong hands

In addition to counting points it is useful to count playing tricks (PT) on strong distributional hands.

Playing tricks are tricks that you expect to make as declarer, assuming that your long suit is trumps and that all suits break normally. A suit such as A-K-Q-J-6-5-3 is worth 7 PT and a suit such as K-Q-J is worth 2 PT.

It is not always easy to evaluate more ragged suits but it is reasonable to hope that partner has a doubleton in your long suit, that you can get into his hand to finesse and that, if two honours are missing, each opponent will have one. A suit such as A-Q-J-x-x-x is worth about 5 PT if opponents' cards split 3-2 and a suit such as Q-J-10-x-x is worth about 2 PT if opponents' cards split 4-2. A-K-J-x-x-x is worth 6PT if the opponents' cards split favourably and the finesse is right.

The opening bid of 2NT

An opening bid of 2NT shows a strong balanced hand of 20-22 points. Like other no-trump bids in Acol it is a limit-bid, and not forcing. Responder can pass, but, with about 4 or more points, should try to find a bid.

Responses to 2NT

With a balanced hand, pass on 0-3 points but raise 2NT quantitatively on stronger hands to 3NT (on 4-10 points) or a slam (on 13-14 points). With a hand that is borderline for a slam response (11-12 points) bid 4NT, a quantitative bid which asks partner to bid 6NT if he is maximum or pass if he is minimum. These responses are based on the assumption that you need at least 33 combined points to make a small slam if you and your partner both have balanced hands.

Just occasionally you will have the strength to contemplate a grand slam when your partner opens 2NT. For this you would require a minimum 37 points in the combined hands. Therefore, if you have at least 17 points you could bid 7NT direct. If you have only 15-16 points you can bid 5NT, which demands that partner should bid 6NT on a minimum or 7NT on a maximum.

A response of 3♣ is conventional and forcing. It is either *Stayman* or (by arrangement) the *Baron 3♣* convention. The Baron 3♣ response asks opener to start showing his biddable suits in ascending order; if opener's only biddable suit is clubs, he bids 3NT. Responder's purpose in bidding 3♣ is to find a major suit fit or the otherwise difficult-to-find minor suit fit. He may be looking for a game or slam and his hand is probably unsuitable for no-trumps. There is no weak take-out over a 2NT opening bid, which means that a response of 3♡ or 3♠ is forcing to game, opener raising to 4 of a major or taking back into 3NT. For years the standard way of stopping in 3♡ or 3♠ has been by way of the *Flint* convention, a response of 3◊, which demands a transfer to 3♡, which can be passed by responder or converted to 3♠ if that is responder's suit. Nowadays more and more players are changing over to *red suit transfer bids*, whereby a response of 3◊ demands a transfer to 3♡ and a response of 3♡ demands a transfer to 3♠. The advantages of transfer bids to describe a wide variety of hands are pointed out by Eric Crowhurst in his *Precision Bidding in Acol*, which any aspiring partnership should consult. For the less committed player, the simple version of the Flint convention given above will probably suffice on the majority of hands.

An immediate response of 4♣ is the Gerber convention (p.74). A response of 4♡ or 4♠ to 2NT is a sign-off, which opener should pass.

Some examples:

♠ A Q 6
♡ K 7 5
◇ A Q 3
♣ A Q J 4

Partner opens 2NT on this hand and you have to respond on the hands below.

(a) ♠ K 7 3
   ♡ 8 6 2
   ◇ 7 5 4 2
   ♣ 9 7 5

(b) ♠ K 7 5 3
   ♡ J 6 2
   ◇ J 10 7
   ♣ 9 5 2

(c) ♠ K 7 3
   ♡ Q 8 2
   ◇ K J 10 4
   ♣ K 9 2

(d) ♠ K 7 3
   ♡ A Q 2
   ◇ J 10 7 4
   ♣ K 5 2

(e) ♠ K 7 3
   ♡ A Q 6
   ◇ K 6 5 4
   ♣ K 6 5

(f) ♠ K 8 7 5 3
   ♡ Q 8 6
   ◇ K 7 5
   ♣ 7 6

(g) ♠ K J 8 5 4 2
   ♡ Q 6
   ◇ K 7 4
   ♣ 8 2

(h) ♠ 9 8 5 4 3 2
   ♡ 6 2
   ◇ 6 4 2
   ♣ 6 5

(i) ♠ K 4 3 2
   ♡ A J 8 2
   ◇ 4
   ♣ K 7 5 2

Answers:

(a) Pass

(b) Raise to 3NT

(c) Bid a quantitative 4NT, inviting 6NT

(d) No messing about… bid 6NT direct

(e) Bid 5NT, which *demands* 6NT and invites 7NT on a maximum

(f) Bid 3♠, demanding 3NT or 4♠

(g) Bid 4♠ direct

(h) Bid 3◇ (Flint convention) and convert partner's forced 3♡ response to 3♠

(i) Bid 3♣ (Baron convention) and if partner responds 3NT, bid 6♣. Note that Stayman would have missed the minor suit fit.

The opening bid of 2♣

2♣ is the strongest opening bid that can be made in the Acol system. It is conventional, not necessarily showing a club suit and, except for the one sequence described below, is unconditionally forcing to game.

There are two types of 2♣ opening bid. 2♣ with a no-trump rebid shows an evenly-balanced hand of at least 23 points. 2♣ with a suit rebid shows a powerhouse hand with a minimum of 9 playing tricks and the shape to make game virtually on its own; 23 points are not required but it is difficult to find a suitable hand without a high point count.

Examples:

♠ A K 4	♠ A K 4	♠ A K Q 7 4 3
♡ K J 10	♡ A J 5	♡ A K 5 4
◊ A Q 6 2	◊ A K 7 4	◊ A Q 7
♣ A Q 8	♣ A Q 3	♣ –
Open 2♣ and rebid 2NT	Open 2♣ and rebid 3NT	Open 2♣ and rebid in spades

Responses to Acol 2♣

The negative response is 2◊, made on weak hands of less than 8 points whether or not they contain a diamond suit. Other suit responses are positive, showing a genuine suit and at least an ace. A response of 2NT shows a balanced hand of at least 8 points and a response of 3NT shows a balanced hand of 10-12 points; this is rare, as such a hand will often qualify for a positive suit response.

As mentioned above, all sequences starting with 2♣ are forcing to game, except one. This is 2♣-2◊-2NT-NB. The 2NT rebid shows a balanced hand of 23-24 points and, if responder is very weak, he can pass. Any other sequence starting with 2♣ must be kept open until game, at least, is reached.

Just one further point; if responder has a positive response and his suit is diamonds, he must respond 3◊, not the negative 2◊.

Opening bids of 2◊, 2♡ or 2♠ (Acol strong two bids)

There are three classes of Acol strong two hands:

1 Strong, distributional hands with one long suit, capable of taking at least eight tricks.

2 Strong two-suiters where, although eight tricks are not obvious, they are likely to develop if played in the best fit.
3 Powerful hands with good shape and a high point count which need to be bid strongly but which lack the 9 playing tricks needed for a 2♣ opener. The indication here is opener's urgent need to ensure himself a rebid.

Strong two bids are unconditionally forcing for one round. When responding to an Acol two bid, a single raise of partner's suit, for example 2♡-3♡, is stronger than the double raise, 2♡-4♡, to allow more space to explore for a possible slam. The single raise agrees the suit (3-card support is adequate) and shows an unlimited hand including at least one ace or void. It is better to support partner's major suit than to show a minor suit of your own. Thus, with

♠ J 9 4
♡ 9
◊ A K Q 7 5 3
♣ 8 6 2

raise 2♠ to 3♠ but bid 3◊ over 2♡.

In the sequence 2♡-4♡ responder shows good trump support and probably about 10 points *but no ace or void.*

A response of 3NT shows a balanced hand of 10-12 points. A response of 2NT is negative, made on weak hands which lack the features needed for a suit response, a raise of partner's suit or a response of 3NT. Responder is forced to bid 2NT even if he has a Yarborough but he can pass opener's rebid if it is not forcing. Opener can force him to bid again by jumping in a new suit, for example 2♣-2NT-4◊, or by reversing, 2◊-2NT-3♡-etc. Even if opener makes a minimum rebid such as 2♡-2NT-3♡, responder should try to keep the bidding open, even on slender values, because of his partner's announced strength.

A sequence that begins with an Acol two bid and a positive response, that is a suit response or a single raise of partner's suit, is forcing to game.

Slam conventions

Strong bidding sequences may lead to a slam, but one must know how many aces and kings the partnership holds, so that two tricks are not lost straightaway on the opening lead.

Blackwood: The Blackwood convention may conveniently be used to find out about partnership aces and kings when a suit has been agreed and a slam is being considered. The bid of 4NT asks partner how many aces he has and he replies on the following scale:

 5♣ = no ace or 4 aces
 5♦ = 1 ace
 5♡ = 2 aces
 5♠ = 3 aces

If all 4 aces are held by the partnership then 5NT can be bid to enquire about kings with replies on the scale:

 6♣ = no king
 6♦ = one king
 6♡ = 2 kings
 6♠ = 3 kings
 6NT = 4 kings

If no suit has been agreed, then Blackwood *cannot* be used. For example, 1♠-3♠-4NT is Blackwood as is 1♠-2♡-4NT because the heart suit has been agreed by inference. However, 1NT-4NT or 2NT-4NT is not Blackwood but a quantitative bid asking opener to bid 6NT on a maximum point count.

One word of caution about Blackwood. If a minor suit has been agreed, the Blackwood slam convention may take the bidding too high in that the responses to the enquiries about aces and kings may commit the partnership to a higher contract than it can make. If there is a risk of this use a cue-bidding sequence (see p.75).

Gerber: If your partner opens 1NT or 2NT you must not use 4NT to ask for aces, as this is a quantitative bid, so you must use 4♣ Gerber instead. This is a conventional bid, asking for aces, and opener replies on the scale:

 4♦ = no ace
 4♡ = one ace
 4♠ = 2 aces
 4NT = 3 aces
 5♣ = 4 aces

It is unusual for a player to introduce Gerber without at least one ace himself so the 5♣ = 4 aces reply is rare and the enquirer can proceed to 5♣ to ask about kings. Replies to the king enquiry are on the same stepwise scale, 5◊ = no king, etc.

Cue-bidding

Slam conventions such as Blackwood or Gerber can tell you how many aces and kings the partnership holds but cue-bidding can reveal which suits they are in, information that may be vital to the bidding of a slam.

When a partnership has agreed a trump suit, a bid of a new suit that commits the partnership to game or a higher level is a cue-bid, showing a control in that suit. By control we mean an ace or a void (first round control) or a king or a singleton (second round control).

However, note the difference between 1♠-2♠-3♣ and 1♠-3♠-4♣. In the first sequence 3♣ is a trial bid (p.61) *inviting a game contract*; in the second sequence 4♣ is a cue-bid, *committing the partnership to game* and investigating a possible slam. Similarly, in a sequence such as 1♠-4♠-5♣ the last bid is a cue-bid, as game has already been reached.

Unpractised partnerships should restrict their *initial* cue-bids to showing first round controls, that is, aces or voids. Second-round controls can be shown later by cue-bidding suits in which a member of the partnership has already shown first-round control or in which the player himself has already denied first-round control by by-passing it in the bidding sequence.

Responses to cue-bids

If responder to the cue-bid is maximum for the bids he has made so far, any forward-going bid by his partner, such as a cue-bid, may incline him to bid the slam direct, particularly if the cue-bid has improved his hand by plugging some weak suit.

If responder is minimum for his previous bidding he will sign off by returning to the agreed trump suit at the lowest possible level.

If responder wishes to investigate further he can make a cue-bid himself, choosing the cheapest available (usually the lowest-ranking side suit in which he holds an ace or void). Or he may be able to make a return cue-bid in the suit his partner has already cue-bid. For example, in the sequence 1♠-3♠-4♣-5♣ the last bid would show second-round control of clubs (the ♣K or a singleton) but the lack of the ◇A or the ♡A, which could have been shown more cheaply.

A combination of Blackwood used sparingly, Gerber over no-trumps and simple cue-bids, should lead the partnership to the right spot on the majority of strong hands.

Suit play

Ruffing in the hand that is shorter in trumps gains extra tricks; ruffing in the long trump hand does not win extra tricks but may be necessary to gain the lead for a finesse or to establish a side suit without losing a trick. On some hands, where dummy's trumps are good, you can make more tricks by taking all the ruffs in declarer's hand and treating dummy as the master trump hand. This play, known as a dummy reversal, has already been discussed (Deal 21).

There are some combinations of cards, for example J-x-x opposite K-x-x, that you should try to avoid leading yourself. If you touch these, you may not win a trick at all, but if the opponents lead the suit you are fairly sure of one trick simply by playing low second in hand. Declarer can sometimes make the opponents lead such a suit by stripping their hands of the other suits before throwing them into the lead. Another case in which the opponent's lead will help you arises when they have to lead a suit in which both you and dummy are void, whilst you still have a trump left in each hand. You can then trump in one hand and discard a loser from the other, a procedure known as a ruff-discard.

♠ A K Q 3   *Deal 31.* What is your opening bid on this hand?
♡ A K J 10 6 3
◇ A
♣ Q 2

The great trick-taking potential makes this a 2♣ opening bid. This is conventional and forcing, and you can show your genuine suit on the next round.

Partner responds 3♣, showing positive values and a biddable club suit. You bid 3♡ and he raises to 4♡. What do you do now?

The knowledge that partner has at least a positive response and support for your hearts is very encouraging. If you want to check aces and kings, you can employ the Blackwood convention, in which case the bidding sequence would be as follows:

The bidding	*You*	*Partner*
	2♣ (forcing)	3♣ (positive response)
	3♡	4♡
	4NT (Blackwood)	5◊ (1 ace)
	5NT	6◊ (1 king)
	7♡	

You make the 5NT enquiry for kings, knowing that you have all four aces between you. Partner's one king must be in a minor suit and it doesn't matter which; if the ♣K you have no club loser, if the ◊K the losing club can be thrown on it.

North leads the ♣8 against West's contract of 7♡. Plan the play.

♠ A K Q 3		♠ 8 5
♡ A K J 10 6 3	N	♡ Q 5 4
◊ A	W E	◊ K 9 3
♣ Q 2	S	♣ A 10 6 5 4

Planning: The potential losers from West's point of view are one spade and one club. The club can be thrown on dummy's ◊K; the spade will have to be ruffed in dummy so you must not draw all the trumps before this has been done.

The play: Go straight up with the ♣A (it could be fatal to try the finesse) and enter your own hand with the ◊A. You can now test the trumps and, if both opponents follow, play a second round but not a third. Play the ♠A-K and the ♠3, ruffing with the ♡Q. Play the ◊K, discarding your ♣Q. Return to your own hand by ruffing a diamond high, draw any trump that remains, and the rest of your cards are winners.

Postscript: The play is only likely to fail if one of the opponents started with a singleton spade and three hearts and was able to trump the second round of spades. Without this misfortune, declarer should make three spades and a spade ruff, six hearts, two diamonds and a club.

♠ A Q J 10 9   *Deal 32. What is your opening bid on this hand?*
♡ A
◊ K Q J 10
♣ 6 4 2

This hand has 17 high card points and one distributional point, for the fifth spade. Spades and diamonds are both strong suits so it is best to count playing tricks before deciding what to open.

The hand is slightly substandard for an Acol two bid, for although it might develop eight tricks (four spades, three diamonds and the ♡A), to open 2♠ and rebid 3◊ would normally show a hand of better shape (6-5 or 6-4).

It is, therefore, best opened 1♠. Partner now raises to 3♠ and you can cue-bid your first-round control of hearts, to explore the possibility of a slam. Partner, having no first-round control (see below), signs off in 4♠. If you had stretched to open 2♠, partner would have raised to 4♠, showing good trump support but no ace or void, and you would not have been tempted to bid on.

The bidding   *You*   *Partner*
                         1♠   3♠
                         4♡   4♠

North leads the ♡6 against West's contract of 4♠. Plan the play.

♠ A Q J 10 9		♠ K 6 5 3
♡ A	N	♡ Q J 8 4
◊ K Q J 10	W E	◊ 6 3
♣ 6 4 2	S	♣ K J 3

Planning: The potential losers are the ◊A and, if the clubs lie badly, three club tricks. However, you will have time to discard two of dummy's clubs on your diamonds and to ruff a club in dummy later.

The play: Win with the ♡A, draw trumps and lead the ◇K to force out the ◇A. If North wins and plays a club, try the ♣J from dummy. South may win with the ♣Q but, if he returns a club, your king will take a trick. Win the lead in whichever suit South returns and lead out all your diamonds, discarding two clubs from dummy. You can then ruff at least one club in dummy to ensure your contract.

Postscript: It is pointless to ruff hearts in your own hand (the long trump hand) as you have already counted your five spades as winners anyway; you might just as well lead spades from your own hand and discard hearts on them. Getting ruffs in the shorter trump hand gives extra tricks and is a superior play to the taking of two club finesses.

♠ K Q J 6   *Deal 33*. Your partner deals and opens 2◇. What
♡ 9 6 3 2   do you respond?
◇ 6 4
♣ A 6 2

Partner's opening bid shows a minimum of eight tricks if diamonds are trumps. You have ample values for a change of suit response, so you bid 2♠. Partner raises to 3♠. What should you do now?

   Partner's agreement of your spade suit is good news and you should make some forward-going move. The best bid is 4♣, a cue-bid, showing first-round control of the suit and slam interest. Instead of bidding 4NT to ask for aces, partner now bids a direct 5NT. This unusual bid is the grand slam force, instructing you to bid 6♣ with none of the top three honours in the trump suit, to bid six of the agreed trump suit if you have one of the top three honours, and with more to bid the grand slam direct. This is a modification of the original grand slam force.

The bidding	*You*	*Partner*
		2◇
	2♠	3♠
	4♣	5NT
	7♠	

North leads the ♡K against West's contract of 7♠. Plan the play.

```
♠ K Q J 6        N        ♠ A 10 4 3
♡ 9 6 3 2                 ♡ A
♦ 6 4        W       E    ♦ A K Q J 7 2
♣ A 6 2          S        ♣ 8 4
```

Planning: Looked at from West's point of view, the potential losers are three hearts and two clubs. If the trumps split 3-2, however, there should be no problem. West can draw trumps in three rounds, run the diamonds, discarding two clubs and two hearts; the remaining heart loser can be ruffed in dummy later.

Play: If one of the opponents shows out on the second round of trumps (trumps split 4-1) then the heart ruff must be taken straightaway before the remaining trumps are drawn.

Postscript: You can make more tricks in the 4-4 spade contract than you can in the 6-2 diamond contract. In spades, the diamond suit provides discards for West's losers but, in diamonds, there is no way of avoiding a losing club.

♠ 7   *Deal 34.* You open 2♡ on this hand and your
♡ A K Q J 4 2   partner responds 3♡. What do you bid now?
♦ K 3
♣ A Q 3 2

You opened 2♡ because the shape of the hand was good and you could count six tricks in hearts, a half trick in diamonds and 1 ½ tricks in clubs. Partner's response of 3♡ is stronger than 4♡; it shows agreement for hearts and an unlimited hand including at least one ace or void. Your next bid should be 4♣, a cue-bid, showing first-round control of clubs, and denying first-round control of spades, which you could have shown more cheaply. Your partner responds 4♦. What should you do now?

The 4♦ bid is also a cue-bid, showing first-round control. This improves your hand greatly and encourages you to make a further effort. One can never cue-bid in the trump suit because partner will take this as a sign-off, but having denied first-round control of spades you are now free to show second-round control. You, therefore, bid 4♠ and your partner responds 5♣. What do you make of that?

Since you have already shown first-round control of clubs, your partner is showing second-round control (the ♣K or a singleton). Therefore you know partner has heart support, first-round control of diamonds and second-round control of clubs. Apart from a possible spade loser, everything looks pretty solid and you should bid 6♡.

The bidding	*You*	*Partner*
	2♡	3♡ (positive response)
	4♣ (1st round control of clubs, denies 1st round control of spades)	4◊ (1st round control)
	4♠ (2nd round control)	5♣ (return cue-bid in clubs showing 2nd round control)
	6♡	NB

So by making the initial cue-bids with first-round controls, the partnership was able to show second-round controls later without ambiguity.

North leads the ♠A-K against West's contract of 6♡. Plan the play.

	N	
♠ 7		♠ 8 6 2
♡ A K Q J 4 2	W E	♡ 10 9 8
◊ K 3		◊ A 10 4 2
♣ A Q 3 2	S	♣ K 7 6

Planning: You have already lost one spade trick and there is a potential loser in clubs. You could hope that the clubs will split 3-3 but this line of play will succeed only about 36 per cent of the time. Or you might draw two rounds of trumps, play off three rounds of clubs and ruff the fourth club with dummy's ♡10. This will fail if one opponent has at least three trumps and only a doubleton club.

Better still, you can play a dummy reversal. Looked at from dummy's point of view there are another two spade losers and two diamond losers, but all these can be ruffed high and the low hearts in the West hand can be used to gain entries back to dummy.

The play: Ruff the ♠K with a high heart, cash the ◊K, then ◊A, and ruff the ◊4 high. Enter dummy with a low club to the ♣K, ruff the ◊10 high. Enter dummy with a low heart to the ♡8, ruff the last spade high. Enter dummy with the ♡9, draw the third round of trumps and cash the remaining clubs.

Postscript: The play succeeds provided that diamonds are no worse than 5-2 and trumps no worse than 3-1. The winners are two spade ruffs, three hearts in dummy, two diamonds, two diamond ruffs and three top clubs. The presence of winning trumps in dummy made the dummy reversal possible.

♠ A K 3 2	*Deal 35.* What is your opening bid on this hand
♡ A Q 5	and what do you bid if your partner responds
◊ A J 3	with a bid of 4♣?
♣ K 3 2	

With a balanced hand of 21 points the correct opening bid is 2NT. Partner's response of 4♣ is the Gerber slam convention, asking about aces. You reply on the stepwise principle, so with three aces your bid is 4NT.

   Partner now bids 5♣, asking for kings. You reply 5♠, showing two kings, and partner bids 6♠, which becomes the final contract.

The bidding	You	Partner
	2NT	4♣
	4NT	5♣
	5♠	6♠

Having discovered, by the use of the Gerber convention, that the partnership was missing one king, your partner decided to settle for 6♠. As you bid spades first (conventionally) you become declarer, although partner has the better spade suit.

North leads the ♣Q against West's contract of 6♠. Plan the play.

♠ A K 3 2		♠ Q J 10 9 5 4
♡ A Q 5	N	♡ 6
◊ A J 3	W E	◊ K 10 2
♣ K 3 2	S	♣ A 5 4

Planning: There is an excellent fit in spades but both hands contain three cards in each minor suit, so minor suit losers can't be ruffed. There are eleven tricks 'on top' and a possible heart or diamond finesse for a twelfth. If only one of the two finesses succeeds, you will make your contract so you have about a 75 per cent chance of success. There is, however, another play that will guarantee success, and that is a throw-in.

The play: Win the lead with the ♣A, draw trumps, play the ♡A, and ruff a heart. Return to your own hand with the ♣K, ruff another heart and get off lead with a low club. The opponent who wins this trick will have to lead a heart, a diamond or a club. If he leads a diamond you will win three tricks in the suit, by playing low second in hand; if he leads a heart or a club you will ruff in one hand and discard a losing diamond from the other hand.

Postscript: The throw-in is infallible provided neither you nor dummy has any hearts or clubs when the opponents are given the lead.

CHAPTER 8
Pre-emptive Bidding

Pre-emption is the act of attacking first, to forestall possible enemy action. To see how this applies to bridge, imagine you have a weak hand with one very long suit. Opponents will then probably also have long suits, with strong point counts and, left to themselves, will conduct a smooth bidding sequence which will take them to game or even, possibly, to a slam. Your aim, therefore, will be to put a spanner in the works by starting the bidding at a high level to rob them of bidding space, so making it difficult for them to find their best contract.

A pre-emptive bid, therefore, is usually made at the three-level or above, on a weak hand with a long suit, in the hope of robbing the opponents of the space to find their optimum contract. The requirements for the bid are a weak one-suited hand, with seven or more cards in the long suit, poor defensive values, and nothing that could provide good support for a possible suit in partner's hand, that is, no 4-card major in addition to the long suit that has been bid.

With regard to playing tricks, you should work to 'the rule of 2 and 3', that is, be prepared to be defeated by two tricks if you are vulnerable (and probably doubled), or by three tricks if you are not vulnerable, in order to prevent opponents from bidding and making a game.

These pre-emptive three openings will be based on about 6 playing tricks if you are not vulnerable and 7 playing tricks if you are vulnerable.

Suitable hands for a three-level pre-emptive opening would be:

♠ 3	♠ A Q J 7 5 3 2	♠ 7 2
♡ A Q 9 8 5 4 3	♡ 9 5 2	♡ 6 5
◊ J 7 2	◊ 9 4	◊ K Q J 10 7 5 2
♣ 6 4	♣ 3	♣ Q 4
Open 3♡	Open 3♠	Open 3◊

BUT: ♠ K J 10 7 5 4   and   ♠ K 7 6 4

♠ K J 10 7 5 4	♠ K 7 6 4
♡ 3 2	♡ A Q J 9 6 4 3
◊ A Q 5	◊ 5 4
♣ 8 5	♣ –
Open 1♠	Open 1♡
(Too strong for 3♠)	(Too strong for 3♡, also there is a 4-card spade suit)

There are two final points about pre-emptive three-bids – they may not work out well if it is partner, not the opponents, who is strong, as you will then have deprived your side of bidding space, not theirs. This will not happen, however, if partner knows the right responses. Also note that a pre-emptive three-bid should not be made fourth in hand after three passes, because it is pointless to risk incurring a penalty against two opponents who have already passed.

Responses to partner's three-bids

As opener is known to be weak, responder will usually pass, hoping that he won't go down too badly. There are, however, from time to time, hands on which responder would genuinely want to make a reply to the pre-emptive opening. The last thing opener requires is trump support, so a doubleton can be considered adequate. You do, though, need 3-4 tricks in the side suits before you raise him to game.

The other type of hand on which you might want to raise partner's suit is with length in his suit and weakness everywhere else. In this case you could well make 'an advance sacrifice' in the hope of deflecting your opponents from a possible slam.

On the other hand, a response of 3NT requires a fit in partner's suit (at least three cards) as without the fit you may never be able to set up his suit and gain entry to his hand to enjoy it. You will also need strong guards in the other suits. A solid suit of your own and strong guards in the other suits would also justify a 3NT response.

You will seldom have the requirements to bid a suit of your own in response to partner's three-bid, but if you want to do this, remember that a change-of-suit to a major is forcing to game, whilst a change-of-suit to a minor suggests a *slam in partner's suit*. Some examples should make this clear:

Partner opens 3♡ (not vul):	♠ A 9 2 ♡ 7 5 ◊ A Q 5 4 2 ♣ Q J 6 Pass and hope he makes 3♡.	♠ A K 6 2 ♡ 10 9 ◊ A K 7 5 ♣ 4 3 2 Raise to 4♡.
	♠ K Q 10 ♡ J 7 2 ◊ A J 9 ♣ A Q 7 4 Take out into 3NT.	♠ A 5 4 ♡ A J 8 ◊ A K Q 10 9 6 ♣ 7 Bid 4◊ suggesting a *heart* slam.

If opponents open three of a suit

Don't be tempted to come into the bidding on slender values because you fear you are missing something. With really good opening bid values, however, you should take some action. You will need to agree one of the accepted take-out conventions with your partner. No method is perfect but the take-out double seems to be gaining in popularity.

The Acol gambling 3NT

A weak hand with an absolutely solid minor suit is nowadays opened with a 'gambling 3NT' in the hope of snatching nine tricks if partner has a couple of tricks in the other suits, or at least in preventing the opponents from reaching a contract of their own. In the old days, the 3NT opening was made with a solid minor suit and about an ace and a king in the side suits, so giving you a good chance of making game.

In recent years, however, the bid has been devalued to the point of needing only the solid minor suit with practically no high cards elsewhere.

Responses to partner's gambling 3NT

You will miss many a good contract if you don't know the responses to this bid, so here is a simple version:

1 Knowing that opener can have at the very most a king outside his running minor, don't leave your partner to struggle in 3NT unless you have guards in the other three unbid suits. If you pass, therefore, it means that you are prepared to play in 3NT.

2 Whether or not you can tell which minor opener has, if you can't stand his bid of 3NT and have no great ambitions, retreat to 4♣.

3 A take-out into 4◊ is used to ask partner to cue-bid any void or singleton he may hold, on the rare occasions when you think a slam may be on.

4 A take-out into four of a major shows a good strong suit in which responder is prepared to play.

5 By agreement, 4NT may be used as a slam try, asking opener to press on if his hand contains an extra trick.

6 An immediate bid of 5♣ facing the 3NT opening shows a hand on which responder wishes to be in game and opener should either pass 5♣ or convert to 5◊ if that is his suit.

7 Finally, if responder has bid 4◊, as in (3), opener's rebids are as follows:

    4♡ = singleton or void in hearts
    4♠ = singleton or void in spades
    4NT = no singleton or void
    5♣ = singleton or void in *diamonds*
    5◊ = singleton or void in *clubs*

Some examples: Partner has opened 3NT.

♠ Q J 10 9 5 3	♠ A K 9	♠ A K Q 8 4
♡ 9 7	♡ K Q J 7	♡ K 5
◊ 5 2	◊ K Q 10 8 6 2	◊ A K Q 7 6
♣ K Q 2	♣ –	♣ 5
Opener's suit must be diamonds but bid 4♣.	Opener can't hold ♡A or ◊A. Convert to 5♣.	Opener can't hold ♡A. Bid 6♣.

♠ A J 10 7 5 4 2   *Deal 36.* What do you open on this hand, not
♡ 7   vulnerable?
◊ K 7 5
♣ 4 3

If you assume that partner has at least a doubleton in your long suit, you should be able to make five or six spade tricks and there is also the chance of making the ◊K. The hand probably contains six playing tricks and is the right shape for a three-level pre-emptive bid. You should, therefore, open 3♠ to prevent the opponents from finding a possible game in one of the other suits. Partner raises to 4♠.

The bidding	*You*	*Partner*
	3♠	4♠

Partner (see the hand shown below) recognised that spades was the right suit as ♠K-3 is excellent support for a pre-emptively bid suit. He knows that the ♠K is worth one trick, and that there is a sure heart trick and two club tricks, so you should have ten tricks between you.

North leads the ♣7 against West's contract of 4♠. Plan the play.

♠ A J 10 7 5 4 2		♠ K 3
♡ 7	N	♡ A 9 2
◊ K 7 5	W E	◊ 9 6 4 2
♣ 4 3	S	♣ A K J 10

Planning: West's potential losers are three diamonds and one spade. The lead could be from a doubleton club or 'top of nothing' and it would be foolish to finesse the ♣J or ♣10 at trick one. At all costs you must keep South out of the lead so that he can't switch to a diamond through your ♢K.

The play: Win the first trick with the ♣A. Take two top spade tricks. You can't risk the spade finesse as North might then switch to a heart, taking out dummy's entry. Suppose that the ♠Q does not drop (North discards). Now you must abandon spades as you can't afford to lose the lead. Enter dummy with the ♣K and lead the ♣J.

If South plays low, discard a diamond; if South covers with the ♣Q, ruff this trick, enter dummy with the ♡A and discard a diamond from your hand on the ♣10. Either way you will reduce your losers to three.

Postscript: The play of the ♣J to trap South's ♣Q with your trumps is another example of a ruffing finesse. Even if North holds the ♣Q you will still obtain one diamond discard on the ♣J and another on the ♣10 later. North can't attack diamonds without giving you a diamond trick.

♠ A Q 2	*Deal 37.* Partner opens 3♠ (not vulnerable). What
♡ K 6	do you respond?
♢ A 7 2	
♣ A K Q 10 3	

Although partner's hand is weak, you have such a good fit for his suit and such powerful outside values that a slam should be possible, even a grand slam if partner has the ♡A or a heart void. So bid 4♣, a minor suit cue-bid, showing first-round control of clubs, and inviting partner to show a first-round control if he has one. Over 4♣ partner bids 4♠, a sign-off, showing no first-round control of diamonds or hearts. What do you bid now?

If partner has seven spades to the king, for example, there are still prospects of a small slam if the club suit can be made to run. Unfortunately, if you bid 6♠ and the opponents lead a heart, you may lose the first two tricks.

However, if you can get the opening lead to come up to, rather than through, your hand, you will have a fair chance of making twelve tricks and the best way to do this is to bid 6NT and to play the contract yourself.

The bidding   You   Partner
                                    3♠

                          4♣   4♠
                          6NT

You could have bid 4NT (Blackwood) over 3♠ to find out if partner had an ace but that would have given up the chance of finding out about a useful heart void.

North leads the ◇Q against West's contract of 6NT. Plan the play.

```
♠ A Q 2        ┌─────────┐      ♠ K J 10 9 8 6 5
♡ K 6          │    N    │      ♡ Q 3
◇ A 7 2        │ W     E │      ◇ 9
♣ A K Q 10 3   │    S    │      ♣ 8 7 5
               └─────────┘
```

Planning: Count your winners in this no-trump contract. If you can bring home seven spades, five clubs and one diamond you will make all thirteen tricks. You must be careful not to lose a club or the opponents will cash their red suit winners.

The play: Win the first trick with the ◇A. Before cashing the spades you must test the clubs by playing the ♣A-K. Then, if North has only one club, you will know that you have to finesse against South's ♣J when you have finished running the spades.

Postscript: It would be careless to assume that the clubs will split 3-2. You must test the suit whilst there is still an entry to dummy.

♠ 6 3   *Deal 38.* What is your opening bid on this hand?
♡ 10
◇ Q 3 2
♣ A K Q J 5 4 3

You might consider opening 3♣ or a higher level pre-empt in clubs. However, the hand is very suitable for an Acol gambling 3NT which forces the opponents, if they wish to compete, to start bidding at the 4-level.

After some thought, partner passes, so the bidding was simply:

                You   Partner
                3NT   NB

and the opponents did not intervene.

Although we have shown you an established system of responses to a gambling 3NT, partner (his hand is shown below) still has a difficult decision. He can tell your suit is clubs and realises that he will never be able to lead them. However, if you have so much as a queen outside clubs there is a 50 per cent chance of the West hand obtaining the lead to run the clubs, and 3NT will probably make. So, with some misgivings, partner passes. His alternative, much safer bid would be 4♣, despite his void, as you would certainly make your club tricks in that contract, but he was reluctant to take you out of a game contract into a part-score.

The contract is 3NT by West. How do you play if North leads (a) the ◊A, (b) the ◊J?

```
♠ 6 3              N        ♠ A 9 8 7 5
♡ 10                        ♡ K J 6 5 3 2
◊ Q 3 2        W      E     ◊ K 8
♣ A K Q J 5 4 3    S        ♣ –
```

The problem in each case is to gain entry to the West hand in order to cash the clubs.

(a) It often pays to lead an ace against a gambling 3NT to see dummy, to get a signal from partner, and to decide which suit to attack. On this hand, however, the lead of the ◊A helps declarer if he is quick enough to unblock dummy's ◊K on the ◊A, so ensuring an entry into the West hand later with the ◊Q.

(b) The lead of the ◊J may have been made from a sequence such as ◊J-10-9-x-x or an internal sequence such as ◊A-J-10-9-x. Declarer should put on the ◊8 from dummy, not the ◊K, hoping that North has the ◊A and that the West hand will win the first trick with the ◊Q. If South has the ◊A and at least one other diamond he can always block the suit by playing the ◊A on the ◊8. If dummy's ◊K is played in an attempt to force out the ◊A, South can duck, saving his ◊A for the second round, again blocking the suit for East-West. This is really a problem for the defence. If you, as South, held the ◊A, would you have got it right?

♠ 5 3 2   *Deal 39. What is your opening bid on this hand?*
♡ K Q J 10 8 6 3 2
◇ –
♣ A 9

You can count seven heart tricks and the ♣A but although you have eight playing tricks you would be most unwise to open 2♡ on this hand. You are very short of high cards and weak in defence and it will pay you to open pre-emptively. You are too strong to open 3♡ and the solution is to open 4♡, a bid that denies more than two defensive tricks. If an opening 3♡ makes life difficult for the opponents, 4♡ should make it impossible.

Partner and both opponents pass.

The bidding	*You*	*Partner*
	4♡	NB

Recognising that your opening bid showed about 7-8 playing tricks but weakness in the other suits, your partner is content to pass. His own values in spades and diamonds (see below) make it unlikely that the opponents could have made game but give you a chance of making your own contract.

North leads the ◇A against West's contract of 4♡. Plan the play.

♠ 5 3 2	N	♠ A Q 8
♡ K Q J 10 8 6 3 2	W E	♡ 7 5 4
◇ –	S	◇ Q J 5 3
♣ A 9		♣ 10 8 6

Planning: There are four potential losers (two spades, one heart and one club). The ♠Q should not be relied on for an extra trick. The lead of the ◇A gives you the chance of setting up a diamond trick, on which a black suit loser can be discarded.

The play: Ruff the diamond lead and play the ♡K to force out the ♡A, hoping that both opponents will follow. If North wins and switches to a spade, go up with the ♠A and lead the ◇Q from dummy to force out the ◇K, discarding a spade from your hand. The opponents can cash only one more spade and you discard a club on the ◇J, after gaining entry to the table with a trump.

Postscript: The discard of a losing spade on the ◊Q is known as 'loser on loser' play. The ◊J is set up and the contract made with seven heart tricks, two black aces and a diamond.

♠ 9 4   *Deal 40.* What is your opening bid on this hand?
♡ 5 4
◊ A
♣ A K J 10 8 6 3 2

The clubs are not solid enough for a gambling 3NT and there is too much strength in the other suits. Obviously you would like to pre-empt, as it is quite possible that the opponents can make a game in one of their suits. You are too good for 3♣, and even 4♣ would be chicken-hearted on this hand. Open 5♣, and if partner has one or two key cards you may even make it. If not, you are almost certainly preventing the opponents from making at least a game.

The bidding   *You*   *Partner*
                       5♣   NB

North leads the ◊K against West's contract of 5♣. Plan the play.

♠ 9 4   ♠ K Q 8 6 2
♡ 5 4   ♡ A Q J
◊ A   ◊ 7 6 5 4
♣ A K J 10 8 6 3 2 ♣ 5

Planning: If you don't lose a club trick the contract is easy, as there is at most one loser in each major suit. If you lose a club trick you will have to play the major suits with care. You have two possible major suit finesses, one against the ♡K and the other against the ♠A, and you have to decide which to try first. If you finesse hearts first and lose to the ♡K the opponents will cash the ♠A to put the contract one down. However, if you try a low spade to the ♠Q or ♠K you can repeat the finesse if it wins, but you still have time to try the heart finesse if it loses.

The play: Win the opening lead with the ◊A and cash the ♣A-K. If the ♣Q fails to fall, switch to a low spade to the ♠Q in dummy. If it wins, return to your hand with a diamond ruff and repeat the spade finesse. If North has the ♠A and plays low again, you will not lose a spade trick; if he plays his ♠A you can discard a heart on the ♠K later. If the spade finesse fails you can regain the lead and try the heart finesse. The contract will make if either finesse succeeds.

Postscript: It would be a mistake to continue with a third club to force out the ♣Q from the North hand, as he might return a heart, making you take the wrong finesse first.

CHAPTER 9

Competition over One No-trump

Many players play the cards quite well as declarer but still make a mess of the defence. Often they fail to realise that the opponents could have been defeated with a different opening lead, or if the defenders had not been in too much of a hurry to snatch their tricks.

In the remaining chapters of this book defensive tactics in bidding are discussed, together with the strategy of opening leads and of signals and discards. These are some of the most rewarding and fascinating areas of the game.

When you compete you will sometimes finish up as declarer, sometimes as defender, so the layout of the hands has to be more flexible than in the earlier chapters.

Doubling the 1NT opening bid

The double of 1NT is for penalties, unlike the double of opponent's suit bid, which is for take-out. To double opponent's 1NT you should have a balanced hand stronger than the opener. The theory behind the double is that, if you are stronger than opener and sit over him, you should defeat the contract provided that partner has his fair share of the remaining points. Thus, if opponents open 1NT on 12-14 points, you should certainly double on a balanced hand of 16 or more points and may double on 15 or even 14 if you have a good suit to lead.

Once the bidding has started with 1NT-Dbl the other two

players can work out which side has the balance of points. If your side is stronger you should try to play in a worthwhile contract (a game or a part-score that will give you game) or to double the opponents if they try to escape into a suit contract. If your side is weaker, you should try to wriggle out of trouble as cheaply as possible, though this may be difficult against keen opposition.

A suit bid over opponent's 1NT

This shows a good suit but not enough strength to double. The hand will be worth five or six playing tricks, assuming the long suit is trumps, but may have only 1-2 tricks in defence. Partner will usually pass but can raise your suit if he has at least a semi-fit (two or three cards to an honour) and strong outside values.

Take-out bids over opponent's 1NT

Most players use bids of 2♣ or 2♢ as conventional take-out bids over opponent's 1NT, asking partner to choose a suit. There are several different versions (Sharples, Astro, Ripstra, Landy, Cansino, etc). If you have not agreed specifically with partner which defensive convention to play, then 2♣ and 2♢ should be treated as natural bids.

Some examples.

Your right-hand opponent opens 1NT (12-14 points).

♠ A 8 4	♠ A 8 4	♠ A K 7	♠ A 9 5
♡ K Q 7 3	♡ K Q J 10	♡ K Q J 4	♡ K Q 7 6 4 2
◊ 5 4 2	◊ Q 10 6	◊ K Q 3	◊ 3
♣ K 10 6	♣ K 10 6	♣ Q 6 2	♣ Q 10 8
Pass	Dbl	Dbl (the Dbl is unlimited)	Bid 2♡

Leading partner's suit against no-trump contracts

If partner has bid, you will often lead his suit against a no-trump contract. With a sequence, lead the top of the sequence; with three or four cards to an honour, lead the lowest card, not the honour; with a doubleton, lead the higher card; with five of his suit (rare), lead the fourth highest (fourth from the top); with three low cards, lead the highest ('top of nothing').

Thus from the following holdings, lead the card underlined:

Q J 10;   K 6 3 2̲;   K 6 3̲;   K 8 6 3̲ 2;   K̲ 6;   6̲ 3;   8̲ 6 2

If your partner leads his own suit against a no-trump contract and you, as third player, win the trick and decide to return the suit, you should return the higher remaining card of an original 3-card holding or the lowest card of an original 4-card holding to give partner a count of the suit. If (rarely) you hold five cards in his suit, you should return the fourth highest card of your original holding. Thus, if partner leads a heart and you win the first trick with your ace, you should return the card underlined.

A 8̲ 4;   A 8 4 2̲;   A 8 6 4̲ 2;   A 6̲ (no choice)

♠ J 10 8 3   *Deal 41.* You are East and neither side is
♡ K 5 3   vulnerable. Your partner (West) opens 1NT (12-
◇ K J 4   14 points) and North doubles. What should you
♣ Q 9 4   bid on this hand?

With 10 high card points in your hand and about 13 points in partner's hand, you might be able to make 2NT but this bid would be madness in these circumstances. If you make eight tricks for 2NT you will score only 70 points, plus the advantage of having a part-score towards game. Your correct action is to redouble. If you make eight tricks you will now score game (160 for 1NT redoubled) plus 200 for the redoubled overtrick and an 'insult bonus' for making a doubled or redoubled contract.

You, therefore, redouble. Your left-hand opponent (South) bids 2♡ and the next two players pass. It is up to you again; what do you bid?

Ask yourself who has the balance of points. Your side has at least 22, their side at most 18. You know that West, North and East have reasonably balanced hands so it is unlikely that South is very distributional. Probably he has bid hearts because he can't stand the thought of you making 1NT redoubled. He is very unlikely to make his 2♡ contract and you should double.

The bidding	West	North	East	South
	1NT	Dbl	Redbl	2♡
	NB	NB	Dbl	All pass

Partner (West) leads the ♣2 against South's contract of 2♡ (doubled). Plan the defence.

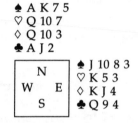

♠ A K 7 5
♡ Q 10 7
◇ Q 10 3
♣ A J 2

♠ J 10 8 3
♡ K 5 3
◇ K J 4
♣ Q 9 4

Partner's lead of the ♣2 is low from an honour, so he must have the ♣Q. Partner must have at least two hearts to open 1NT so declarer has at most five hearts. Partner has at least 12 points for his opening bid, you have 10 and dummy 16, so the most declarer can have is 2 points.

Now that you have a good picture of declarer's hand, it shouldn't be hard to find the right defence. Declarer has no long suits to set up so you need be in no hurry to snatch your winners. You should merely avoid leading suits that may give the other side extra tricks. Trumps are safe for you to lead since partner must have the ♡A and spades are safe, as partner has the ♣Q. If declarer ruffs spades in his own hand this does not give him extra tricks. Your plan is to keep leading the major suits and let declarer struggle with the minor suits himself.

You can't take the first trick but you can signal to partner that you would like him to lead spades again by playing the ♠8 (a high card encourages) not the ♠3 (a low card discourages). Later, when partner gains the lead, he can exit with a spade, which he knows is safe, once he has seen your encouraging signal.

The full deal:

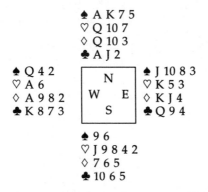

```
              ♠ A K 7 5
              ♡ Q 10 7
              ◇ Q 10 3
              ♣ A J 2
  ♠ Q 4 2                    ♠ J 10 8 3
  ♡ A 6          N          ♡ K 5 3
  ◇ A 9 8 2    W   E        ◇ K J 4
  ♣ K 8 7 3       S         ♣ Q 9 4
              ♠ 9 6
              ♡ J 9 8 4 2
              ◇ 7 6 5
              ♣ 10 6 5
```

North-South will be able to make only two spades, three hearts and the ♣A. Provided the defenders avoid giving away a free gift (that is, they avoid leading a club) declarer will be two down doubled.

Postscript: It may be dangerous to play the weak no-trump but it's dangerous to play against it too. North was correct to double but unlucky to find his partner so weak.

♠ 10 8 7 6   *Deal 42.* You hold this hand as East. Your left-
♡ K 7 2   hand opponent (South) opens 1NT (12-14 points),
◇ J 10 3   your partner doubles and the next player passes.
♣ 9 5 3   What do you bid?

This is an awkward situation. If partner's double is minimum the opponents may have more than 20 points between them and may make their contract. On the other hand, your partner may be stronger – his double is unlimited.

You might consider bidding a 5- or 6-card suit in this situation but, with such a balanced hand, there is no point in disturbing the double. If you do bid a suit, the opponents may double you and defeat the contract. You should, therefore, pass and defend vigorously. Even if 1NT doubled is made, worse things have happened at sea!

The bidding	*South*	*West*	*North*	*East*
	1NT	Dbl	All pass	

Winning Ways at Bridge

As you await the opening lead you expect that partner will either try to find something safe (top of a sequence, perhaps) or will try to set up his own long suit, relying on his high cards as entries.

West (your partner) leads the ♡5 against South's contract of 1NT (doubled), and the ♡3 is played from dummy. Plan the defence.

```
        ♠ K 9 2
        ♡ 6 3
        ◊ Q 7 6 5
        ♣ J 10 7 4
                      ♠ 10 8 7 6
             N        ♡ K 7 2
        W         E   ◊ J 10 3
             S        ♣ 9 5 3
```

Partner has presumably led from his long suit and you must play the ♡K to prevent declarer winning the trick cheaply. This wins the trick and now the right card to return is the ♡7 not the ♡2, to give partner a count of the suit. Declarer plays the ♡4 on the first trick and the ♡8 on the second trick, which partner wins with the ♡9. Because East returned his middle card, West now realises that East started with three and declarer with four. He thus resists the temptation to cash the ♡A, which would present declarer with a trick, and switches to a diamond.

The full deal:

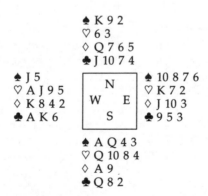

```
            ♠ K 9 2
            ♡ 6 3
            ◊ Q 7 6 5
            ♣ J 10 7 4
   ♠ J 5                    ♠ 10 8 7 6
   ♡ A J 9 5      N         ♡ K 7 2
   ◊ K 8 4 2   W     E      ◊ J 10 3
   ♣ A K 6         S        ♣ 9 5 3
            ♠ A Q 4 3
            ♡ Q 10 8 4
            ◊ A 9
            ♣ Q 8 2
```

Each time West gains the lead with a club, he continues with a low diamond to create an entry to the East hand so that the ♡2 can be led through South's ♡Q-10 to West's ♡A-J.

On this defence declarer will make only three spade tricks and two diamonds, whilst the defence will make four heart tricks, two diamonds and two clubs, to put the contract two down.

♠ 8 2　　　　　*Deal 43. You are West and hold this hand. Your*
♡ A 5 3 2　　*left-hand opponent (North) opens 1◊, your*
◊ 9 5 3　　　*partner overcalls with 1♠, your right-hand*
♣ 10 8 4 3　　*opponent (South) bids 2NT and North raises to*
　　　　　　　　3NT. What do you lead?

The bidding	*North*	*East*	*South*	*West*
	1◊	1♠	2NT	NB
	3NT	All pass		

South's bid of 2NT over your partner's spade call indicates that he has good spades sitting over partner, so should you be put off from leading a spade? In some circumstances you might be, for example if you had a singleton spade and a really promising suit of your own. However, this does not apply to this hand and a spade is the obvious lead. Even in borderline cases one should err on the side of leading partner's suit rather than your own, on the theory that a primary purpose of making an overcall is to indicate a good lead, and that players should not overcall in suits they don't want led.

You lead the ♣8 against South's contract of 3NT. East plays the ♣9 and South wins with the ♣Q. South now leads the ♡4. Plan the defence.

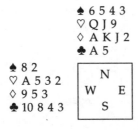

```
              ♠ 6 5 4 3
              ♡ Q J 9
              ◊ A K J 2
              ♣ A 5
♠ 8 2             N
♡ A 5 3 2      W     E
◊ 9 5 3           S
♣ 10 8 4 3
```

If South has about 11 points for his 2NT response, that leaves about 10 points for East. East must have at least a 5-card spade suit and South will probably have the doubleton ♠A-Q sitting over him. East won't have many entries to his hand and these must be preserved until after the ♠A has been forced out. You must, therefore, go up with the ♡A straightaway, and lead another spade to clear the suit, trusting that your partner can get in later to cash his winners.

South's response of 2NT may not be to everyone's taste (see full hand below) but the resulting game contract can easily be made if the defence is careless.

The full deal:

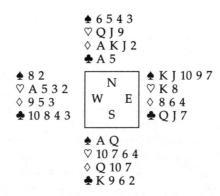

```
                    ♠ 6 5 4 3
                    ♡ Q J 9
                    ◊ A K J 2
                    ♣ A 5
   ♠ 8 2                            ♠ K J 10 9 7
   ♡ A 5 3 2          N             ♡ K 8
   ◊ 9 5 3         W     E          ◊ 8 6 4
   ♣ 10 8 4 3         S             ♣ Q J 7
                    ♠ A Q
                    ♡ 10 7 6 4
                    ◊ Q 10 7
                    ♣ K 9 6 2
```

Looking at all four hands one can see that a spade lead was essential for the defence; partner overtook your ♠8 in case it was a singleton. With two tricks in spades, four in diamonds and two in clubs, declarer needed one heart trick for his contract. If you made the mistake of playing low on the first heart, partner would have won with the ♡K and continued spades, but the next heart trick would have come to your ♡A and you would have had no more spades to lead.

♠ 10 6 5   *Deal 44.* You are West. Your left-hand opponent
♡ 10 5 4   (North) opens 1NT (12-14 points) and your
◊ A 8 6   partner doubles. South now bids 2♡. What do you
♣ K 8 7 2   bid?

As partner's double is presumed to be a good 15 points you know that your side is the stronger. You may be able to make a game if partner is more than minimum but you can't be sure of that. However, you can be sure that the opponents are out of their depth and a double is the obvious bid. It's a pity your own trumps are so weak but that should not deter you; partner may have some values in this suit for his double of 1NT and, even if he hasn't, the opponents can't make their contract on trumps alone.

The bidding	*North*	*East*	*South*	*West*
	1NT	Dbl	2♡	Dbl
	All pass			

What is your opening lead against 2♡ doubled?

It doesn't pay to underlead aces against suit contracts, so a diamond lead is out. A spade or a club may work out well but might help declarer, so a trump seems by far the safest. True it may help declarer to find a missing honour in the suit but he could probably have finessed it for himself anyway. You won't mind trumps being drawn and the contract played along no-trumps lines, where your side's overwhelming strength will crush the opponents.

The full deal:

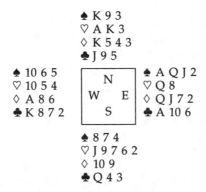

```
               ♠ K 9 3
               ♡ A K 3
               ◇ K 5 4 3
               ♣ J 9 5
   ♠ 10 6 5                    ♠ A Q J 2
   ♡ 10 5 4        N           ♡ Q 8
   ◇ A 8 6    W       E        ◇ Q J 7 2
   ♣ K 8 7 2      S            ♣ A 10 6
               ♠ 8 7 4
               ♡ J 9 7 6 2
               ◇ 10 9
               ♣ Q 4 3
```

Declarer plays dummy's ♡A-K, dropping your partner's ♡Q, so he makes five heart tricks and a diamond later. Being short of entries to his own hand, declarer would probably have played the hearts the same way even if you had not led them. A club lead would have presented declarer with a trick. In the circumstances, it is better for West to find a safe lead that does not risk giving a trick away.

Postscript: Careful defence restricts declarer to six tricks, a good result for East-West as they can't make a game in spades or no-trumps.

♠ 10 8 6	*Deal 45.* You hold this hand as East. Your left-
♡ A 10 8	hand opponent (South) opens 1NT (12-14 points)
♢ J 7 5	and your partner (West) doubles. North now bids
♣ K 6 4 2	2♣. What do you bid?

Most players agree that, after 1NT-Dbl, the 2♣ response is no longer Stayman but shows a genuine club suit. East should reason that his side has the balance of the points and that 2♣ is not going to make. On this hand East's clubs are good too and he should double.

After East's double, the next two players pass and North redoubles. What should you make of this?

The bidding	South	West	North	East
	1NT	Dbl	2♣	Dbl
	NB	NB	Redbl	?

Something strange is going on, but if you were happy with 2♣ doubled, you should be even happier with 2♣ redoubled, so you should pass. South now bids 2♢ and the next two players pass, so it is back to you again. What is your next move?

The bidding	South	West	North	East
	1NT	Dbl	2♣	Dbl
	NB	NB	Redbl	NB
	2♢	NB	NB	?

Don't make the mistake of passing or bidding no-trumps. That 2♣ bid was phoney, the redouble was for SOS. The opponents are on the run and can't make anything. They are just wriggling to find the cheapest spot. You mustn't let them off the hook. You must double them and extract the maximum penalty.

The full deal:

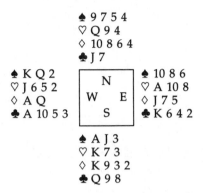

♠ 9 7 5 4
♡ Q 9 4
◇ 10 8 6 4
♣ J 7

♠ K Q 2
♡ J 6 5 2
◇ A Q
♣ A 10 5 3

♠ 10 8 6
♡ A 10 8
◇ J 7 5
♣ K 6 4 2

♠ A J 3
♡ K 7 3
◇ K 9 3 2
♣ Q 9 8

In their diamond contract North-South should lose at least two tricks in each suit. The only point for the defence to watch is that if West leads a heart at some stage, and North plays low, East must play the ♡8, allowing South's ♡K to make but keeping the ♡A-10 sitting over the ♡Q-9 to make two tricks later. To play the ♡A automatically as third player will result in both the ♡K and ♡Q making for North-South.

Postscript: It may seem hard for East to keep track of this involved bidding sequence, but players who habitually use the weak no-trump are good at wriggling out of trouble. All East has to do is to bear in mind that his side has the balance of points and ensure that the opponents don't get away with a cheap save. A safe lead and a careful defence will then reap its reward.

CHAPTER 10

Competition Over Suit Bids

When the opponents have opened one of a suit, your main options are to overcall in your own suit, to bid 1NT, to double (for take-out) or to pass.

The suit overcall

There are many good reasons for getting into the bidding if you can. First, you may be able to interfere with the opponents' bidding sequence, making it difficult for them to reach their best contract. Second, there are many deals on which both sides can make a contract of their own, for example, they can make 4♡ but you can make 4♠. Third, your bid may prepare the way for a sacrifice for your side, for example, you bid 4♠ and go down to prevent them making 4♡. Fourth, your bid may enable partner to double the opponents if they stretch too far. Fifth, you may be able to deflect the opponents from a no-trump contract that they might have made if you had not interfered. Sixth, and perhaps most important of all, your bid will tell partner what to lead if your side defends.

It follows that an overcall should be based on a good suit of at least 5-card length, one that you want led. Partners who overcall on a suit headed only by the jack are best avoided. An overcall is not the same as an opening bid and the accent is on the suit, rather than on the points. To see if your hand qualifies for an overcall, count your playing tricks as explained on p.69. You need to be within three tricks of your contract, not vulnerable, and within two tricks of your contract if vulnerable. With seven or more playing tricks and a 6-card suit you are strong enough to make a jump overcall, for example 2♡ over 1◇, or 3◇ over 1♠.

Some examples:

♠ K 4 2	♠ 8 4 2	♠ A 3
♡ K Q J 10 2	♡ A 7 3	♡ K 7
◇ 9 7 3	◇ 6	◇ A Q J 9 8 6
♣ 8 6	♣ A J 10 9 3 2	♣ K 4 2
Bid 1♡ over opponent's 1♣ or 1◇ but pass over 1♠ (4 ½ PT)	Overcall any 1-bid with 2♣ (5-6 PT)	Make a jump overcall (3◇ over 1♡) (7 PT plus a 6-card suit)

If your partner makes an overcall, your first consideration should be whether or not you can raise his suit. Trump support is what he wants to hear, reassuring him that the trumps are not stacked by the opponent sitting over him. Three-card trump support is ample because partner must have at least a 5-card suit. However, don't make the mistake of raising him to too high a level. Although his suit will be good, his hand won't be very strong, particularly if his overcall has been made at the one-level and your side is not vulnerable. For example, if partner overcalls opponent's 1♣ with 1♠ you should raise him to 2♠ on the following hand:

♠ Q 6 3
♡ A 8 2
◇ K Q 7 3
♣ 8 6 5

Raise partner's 1♠ overcall to 2♠. Partner's spades will be good but his hand will not be very strong, because he couldn't double or jump to 2♠. You can raise on a 3-card trump fit because the overcall will have been made on a 5-card suit.

The 1NT overcall

The overcall of 1NT is always strong and is made on hands of 15-17 (or by partnership agreement 16-18) points, with a good stop (preferably a double stop) in the opponent's suit. A suitable hand would be:

♠ A Q 3
♥ K 9 7 2
♦ K 10 9
♣ K J 8

Overcall any one-level suit bid by the opponents with a bid of 1NT. The overcall must be strong because opener's partner can easily calculate who has the balance of points and is in a good position to double for penalties.

If your partner overcalls with 1NT you should respond as if he had opened the bidding with a strong no-trump. Thus with a balanced hand you would either pass or raise no-trumps; with an unbalanced hand you would either jump to game in a suit, bid 3 of a suit (forcing), or if weak, simply bid 2 of your long suit. It is for each partnership to agree if a response of 2♣ is the Stayman convention or a weakness response on a long club suit, in this situation.

The take-out double

The double of an opponent's suit bid is for *take-out*. It shows a hand of at least opening bid strength, a weakness in opponents' suit but support for the other three suits. With a doubleton in the opponents' suit you could make a take-out double on about 14 or more points; with a singleton in their suit you could double on about 12 points upwards; but with three cards in the opponents' suit you would need about 16 or more points because the extra cards in their suit are a liability. Suitable hands for a double of opponents' 1♥ bid are:

♠ A Q 6 4	♠ A Q 6 4	♠ A Q 6 4
♥ 2	♥ 6 2	♥ 6 4 2
♦ K 9 6 2	♦ K 9 8 2	♦ K Q 8
♣ Q J 10 3	♣ K Q 3	♣ K Q 3

All three hands are about equivalent in playing strength. The double is unconditionally forcing for one round and demands that doubler's partner bids his best suit even if he has no points at all. If, however, the opener's partner bids, then the bidding will come back round to doubler and the doubler's partner is not forced to bid if he has nothing useful to say. However, he should try to find a bid if he has a few points and thinks he can make a better choice than his partner. Because, if your partner doubles and the third player passes you are forced to bid even with no points, it stands to reason that with some points you must jump the bidding to show you have a genuine holding. A shapely hand with values for an opening bid may qualify for a direct jump to game. Thus, if partner doubles 1♡:

♠7 5 3 2	♠K J 5 3 2	♠K Q 7 5 3 2
♡8 5 3	♡J 8 3	♡5 3
◇6 4 3	◇A 4 3	◇A J 3
♣6 5 2	♣3 2	♣3 2
Bid 1♠	Bid 2♠	Bid 4♠

The pass

If the opponents have opened the bidding and your hand is unsuitable for a suit overcall, a 1NT overcall or a take-out double, then you will have to pass, even on a hand that might have qualified for an opening bid if you could have got there first. This is one of the most difficult lessons to learn.

For example, if opponents open 1◇ and you hold one of the following hands:

♠A 6 5	♠A Q J 10 6	♠A J 8 4	♠A J 7
♡K J 5 3	♡K 4 3	♡K 6 5 4	♡K 6 5
◇A Q 6	◇7 3	◇6 4	◇Q 7 3
♣K 10 5	♣8 7 4	♣A Q 9	♣A 8 7 4
Bid 1NT	Bid 1♠	Double	No bid

The fourth hand lacks the strength for a 1NT overcall, the playing tricks for a suit overcall or the shape for a take-out double; having nothing useful to say, say nothing! Remember that your partner still has a bid and can take some action if the bidding looks like dying at a low level; his possible actions are dealt with in the section on 'Protection' (Chapter 11).

♠A J 10 3	*Deal 46.* You are West. Your right-hand opponent
♡K 7 6	(South) opens 1◇. What do you bid on this hand?
◇A 10 7	
♣K 10 9	

With a sound 15 points and a stop in the opponents' suit, you can risk an overcall of 1NT if you don't feel you can double. North passes and your partner bids 3NT.

The bidding	South	West	North	East
	1◊	1NT	NB	3NT

With 10 points himself (see below), partner knows that there are at least 25 points in the combined hands, and responds as he would have done to an opening bid of a strong no-trump.

North leads the ♡Q against West's contract of 3NT. South wins with the ♡A and switches to the ◊K. Plan the play.

♠ A J 10 3		♠ K Q
♡ K 7 6	N	♡ 8 5 4 2
◊ A 10 7	W E	◊ 9 6 5 2
♣ K 10 9	S	♣ A J 2

Planning: North's failure to lead his partner's suit probably means that he has at most a singleton diamond. Now that the ♡A has been played, you can be sure of one heart trick plus four spades and one diamond. You need three club tricks, a certainty if you can make the opponents open up the suit.

The play: Win South's diamond switch with the ◊A. Cash the ♡K and four spade tricks. If South has no spades left, throw him in with the ◊10; if he attempts to cash more diamond tricks he will set up a winner for you and if he leads a club you will make three club tricks. If North has no spades left, throw him in with a heart; he can't have more than three heart winners and, having no spades or diamonds, will have to open up the clubs, which is just what you want.

Postscript: Provided North has no more than a singleton diamond, the throw-in will work against either opponent. You merely have to choose the one with no remaining spades to cash.

♠ Q 9 8	*Deal 47*. You are West. Your left-hand opponent
♡ K Q 10 2	(North) opens 1◊. Your partner doubles and the
◊ J 5 3	next player passes. What do you bid on this hand?
♣ Q 5 3	

Partner's double is for take-out. He has weakness in diamonds but support for the other three suits. After South's pass you would have to bid even if you had no points at all, so with your useful values you will have to jump the bidding. You, therefore, bid 2♡ and your partner, being quite strong for his double (see below) raises you to 4♡.

The bidding	North	East	South	West
	1◊	Dbl	NB	2♡
	NB	4♡		

North leads the ◊A-K against West's contract of 4♡, South following with the ◊7 and then the ◊4. North continues with the ◊Q. Plan the play.

♠ Q 9 8	N	♠ A K 3 2
♡ K Q 10 2	W E	♡ A J 7 3
◊ J 5 3	S	◊ 9 2
♣ Q 5 3		♣ K J 8

Planning: In a suit contract, count the losers from declarer's point of view. You have already lost two diamonds and will lose a club, so you must make sure that you don't lose a third diamond trick now.

The play: Trump the third diamond high, draw trumps and force out the ♣A. You should then make three spades, four hearts, one diamond ruff and two club tricks.

Postscript: South's play of the ◊7 followed by the ◊4 was a 'peter' or 'echo', probably indicating a doubleton diamond and encouraging continuation of the suit. You must avoid the mistake of ruffing the third diamond low or South will over-ruff. Provided trumps break 3-2 as they will about two-thirds of the time, your contract will be safe.

♠ K J 10 9
♡ 6 2
◊ 10 7 6
♣ 10 8 4 2

Deal 48. You are West. Your left-hand opponent (North) opens 1◊ and your partner bids 2◊. South now bids 4◊. What do you bid on this hand?

First, what does partner's 2◊ bid mean? This cue-bid of opponent's suit traditionally shows a very powerful hand with support for the three other suits, a 'super' take-out double. In the old days it used to guarantee first-round control of the opponent's suit and be absolutely forcing to game. Nowadays a jump cue-bid (e.g. 3◊ over 1◊) would be used to show such a hand and the simple cue-bid shows considerable strength but does not necessarily guarantee first-round control of the suit bid.

The 4◊ bid by South is probably pre-emptive, made to prevent East-West from reaching their best contract. Let's suppose that West now bids 4♠, North competes with 5◊ and East bids 5♠.

The bidding	North	East	South	West
	1◊	2◊	4◊	4♠
	5◊	5♠	All pass	

Cautious players might make only a take-out double on the East hand (see below) though optimists might make the jump cue-bid. Partner chose the middle course in making a simple cue-bid. He does have first-round control of diamonds but perhaps not the overall power to guarantee game if you were very weak.

North leads the ♡9 against West's contract of 5♠. Plan the play.

```
        ♠ K J 10 9              ♠ A Q 4 3
        ♡ 6 2        N         ♡ A Q J 10
        ◊ 10 7 6   W   E       ◊ —
        ♣ 10 8 4 2    S        ♣ K Q J 9 7
```

Planning: That heart lead looks ominous. Possibly it is from a doubleton or the 'top of nothing' and it looks as if South may have the ♡K. The losers, from declarer's point of view, are one heart, one club and three diamonds. However, two diamonds can be thrown on the hearts and the remaining one on the clubs. The winners will be four spades, three hearts and four clubs.

The play: Go up with the ♡A and draw trumps, hoping for a 3-2 spade split. Now lead another heart. South can win with the ♡K and if he leads a diamond, you can ruff it in dummy and discard your other two diamonds on the hearts. If he leads a club you will lose the ♣A but will then have enough winners in dummy to discard all your losers.

Postscript: There were two aspects that needed careful play. First, you must not risk the heart finesse at trick one, for if it loses, the opponents will switch to a club, making the ♣A, and a club ruff! Secondly, having drawn trumps you have to establish hearts before clubs because you need two discards quickly and clubs can provide only one. Thus, if you play on clubs first, the opponents will lead a diamond, removing dummy's last trump; then you can discard only one diamond on the clubs and will still have a diamond loser left when the opponents gain the lead with the ♡K.

♠ K Q 10 9 3   *Deal 49.* You are West, with your side not
♡ K 8 2   vulnerable. Your right-hand opponent (South)
♢ 7 3 2   opens 1♢. What do you bid on this hand?
♣ K 4

When considering an overcall, count your playing tricks, *not* your points. Assume that your partner has a small doubleton in your long suit and that the opponents' cards split normally. Also assume average luck with regard to the position of the opponents' high cards so that about half your finesses will work. Your hand, therefore, is worth about four playing tricks, counting 3 PT for the spades and ½ PT for each king. Not vulnerable, you are strong enough to overcall 1♢ with 1♠. Partner raises to 2♠ and all pass.

The bidding	*South*	*West*	*North*	*East*
	1♢	1♠	NB	2♠

Your overcall guarantees a 5-card suit, so partner has excellent support with three to the ace (see below) and is correct to raise your suit. As you have merely made a non-vulnerable one-level overcall you may be quite weak, so partner raises you only to 2♠.

North leads the ♢10 against West's contract of 2♠. South cashes the first three diamond tricks and then plays the ♡A-Q. You win the ♡Q with the ♡K. Plan the play.

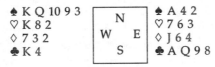

♠ K Q 10 9 3   N   ♠ A 4 2
♡ K 8 2   W   E   ♡ 7 6 3
♢ 7 3 2   S   ♢ J 6 4
♣ K 4   ♣ A Q 9 8

Planning: You have lost four tricks already but if trumps break reasonably you should have no problem in making nine tricks (five trumps, one heart and three clubs). It will cost nothing to play the trumps carefully, so that you don't lose a trick even if South has four to the jack.

The play: Having won the fifth trick with the ♡K, play the ♠K first, then a low trump to the ♠A. If North shows out on the second round, you are in the right hand to finesse against South's ♠J by leading a low trump back towards your ♠Q-10-9. But what if South, not North, discards on the second round of trumps? Now you will lose a trump trick to North , but you need not lose the contract. Abandon trumps and play three rounds of clubs, discarding your last heart; if North trumps he will give up his natural trump trick and your losers will be confined to one heart, three diamonds and one club ruff.

Postscript: If South has four trumps to the jack you can make nine tricks by playing as suggested. If North has four trumps to the jack, you will go down if you play a fourth round whilst you still have a heart loser in your hand.

♠ 4 3   *Deal 50.* You are West, not vulnerable. Your right-
♡ A K Q J 6 3   hand opponent (South) bids 1♠. What do you bid
◊ A Q 7   on this hand?
♣ 6 2

Again, for an overcall, count your playing tricks, not your points. If partner has a doubleton heart you expect to make all six heart tricks and your diamonds are worth 1 ½ PT making 7½ PT in all.

With such power you must make a jump overcall, 3♡ over 1♠. Partner raises you to 4♡ and all pass.

The bidding	*South*	*West*	*North*	*East*
	1♠	3♡	NB	4♡

Partner is right to forget about his club suit (see over) and to raise your hearts instead. His ♡10-5 is adequate support for a suit in which you have made a jump overcall, which shows a 6-card suit. Whatever contract the hand is played in, partner's clubs are worth two sure tricks and, if the suit is established, many more. Failing that, there is the possibility of a diamond ruff, so 4♡ is a reasonable prospect.

North leads the ♡7 against West's contract of 4♡. Plan the play.

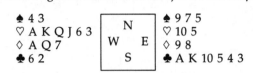

♠ 4 3
♡ A K Q J 6 3
◇ A Q 7
♣ 6 2

♠ 9 7 5
♡ 10 5
◇ 9 8
♣ A K 10 5 4 3

Planning: Count the losers from West's point of view. Two in spades and possibly two in diamonds. If the opponents had not led a trump you would have been able to ruff a diamond in dummy but it's too late for that now because North can lead a second trump when he gains the lead with the ◇K. Your best chance lies in establishing dummy's club suit and discarding your diamonds on clubs.

The play: Draw the trumps and play the ♣2 from your hand and the ♣3 from dummy. South will win and may cash two spades and then lead a diamond. If so, play the ◇A and then lead a club to the ♣A and ♣K. Provided clubs break 3-2 you will be able to discard your losing diamonds, so losing only two spades and a club.

Postscript: The problem was to keep entries to dummy for the club suit. The play of a low club from both hands gave the best chance of doing this.

CHAPTER 11

Protection

Protection is one of the most misunderstood sections of defensive bridge.

The last chapter described the options open to you if the opponents have already opened the bidding, and it was pointed out that, on hands that are not suitable for a 1NT overcall, a take-out double or a suit overcall, you may have to pass even when you have useful values. There is no risk that your side will miss a contract provided that your partner knows how to 'protect'. Thus in the sequence:

West	North	East	South
1◇	NB	NB	?

the fourth player, South, is in the protective position. He should reason that, if West could open with only a one-level bid and East could not reply, then North (his partner) must have reasonable values but was unable to find a sensible bid over 1◇. It is, therefore, up to South to try to find a bid to protect the assumed values in his partner's hand. In this position, eight or more points are enough for a one-level overcall, and the bid can even be made on a 4-card suit. A protective overcall at the two-level would require about 10 or more points and a 5-card suit. The 1NT overcall in the protective position is similarly devalued to about 11-14 points (some partnerships use 10-13) and the only reasonably strong bids in the protective position are take-out doubles or cue-bids of the opponents' suit.

In the example given above, if South bids a suit, then North must allow for the fact that South may be quite weak, and resist any temptation to 'make up for having passed on a good hand'. He should appreciate that South has already bid *both* hands and should try to keep the bidding low.

There are a few words of warning that should be added about protective bids. It sometimes does not pay to protect against really weak opponents who might pass their partner's opening bid on hands on which they should have made responses. This is particularly true if the opening bid was 1♣, which may be a 'prepared' or 'phoney' club, when to protect will merely give opener a chance to escape into a better contract. Don't protect if the suit bid against you is your own best suit and finally, if the bidding goes:

West	North	East	South
1NT	NB	NB	?

it is a mistake for South to lower the requirements for a penalty double. Remember East may have passed on up to 10 points (p.22) so South must keep his double fully up to strength.

♠ A J 10   *Deal 51*. You are West. Your left-hand opponent
♡ A J 2   (North) opens 1♡ and the next two players pass.
◇ 8 6 3   What do you bid on this hand?
♣ Q J 9 8

You are in the protective position. North was able to open only at the one-level and South was too weak to make even a simple response, so your partner (East) is marked with some strength. With a balanced hand and a guard in the opponent's suit you should make an overcall of 1NT in this position.

North passes and your partner raises to 2NT. What now? You could be much weaker than you are. Some players would bid 1NT in the protective position with only 10 points. With 13 points you are near the top of your range and should now bid 3NT.

The bidding	North	East	South	West
	1♡	NB	NB	1NT
	NB	2NT	NB	3NT

With 11 points and a good 5-card suit, partner (see over) realised that there was a chance of game if you were maximum, and explored the possibility with a bid of 2NT, rightly considering that a no-trump game was better than a diamond contract.

North leads the ♡K against West's contract of 3NT. Plan the play.

```
        ♠ A J 10        ┌───────┐      ♠ 9 7 6
        ♡ A J 2         │   N   │      ♡ 7 6 5
        ◊ 8 6 3         │ W   E │      ◊ A K J 7 2
        ♣ Q J 9 8       │   S   │      ♣ K 10
                        └───────┘
```

Planning: The danger suit is hearts and North must be prevented from establishing the suit whilst he still has entries in his hand. Given time, you should be able to set up three club tricks and four diamonds plus a trick in each major suit.

The play: Duck the first heart (the 'Bath Coup'). If North continues with the suit he will give you two heart tricks. Suppose he switches to a diamond. Go up with the ◊A and play on clubs, first the ♣K and then the ♣10, overtaking in your hand and continuing the suit until the ♣A is forced out. You still have the major suits stopped and you can afford to lose a diamond trick to South later.

Postscript: You must not play the ♡A at trick one or South will lead a heart through your ♡J-2 into North's remaining ♡Q-10-x-x when he wins a diamond trick. Also you must not finesse a diamond at trick two. If South wins and leads a heart, your heart stop will be forced out whilst North still has an entry with the ♣A. The principles are similar to those of Deals 6 and 9.

```
♠ A 10 9 8 6    Deal 52. You are West. Your right-hand opponent
♡ 7 6 2         (South) opens 1♡. You pass. North passes and
◊ 10 8 6        East bids 1NT. South passes. What do you bid?
♣ A 9
```

Partner has a balanced hand for his 1NT overcall but, as he was in the protective position, he may have no more than 11 points. It's a close decision on your hand whether you should pass or bid 2♠. If you pass and partner can set up the spade suit, he may make 1NT. If the spades go badly and the opponents lead a club to remove your entry, then 1NT may come unstuck and 2♠ may be a safer contract. Let us assume that you decide to bid 2♠.

The bidding	South	West	North	East
	1♡	NB	NB	1NT
	NB	2♠	All pass	

North leads the ♡3 against West's contract of 2♠. Plan the play.

♠ A 10 9 8 6		N	♠ K 5 3
♡ 7 6 2			♡ K 10 4
◊ 10 8 6	W	E	◊ A Q J 9
♣ A 9		S	♣ 10 6 3

Planning: First, count your losers in this suit contract. One in clubs, one in diamonds if South has the ◊K, one in spades assuming normal breaks and three in hearts, bearing in mind that South bid the suit. However, one heart loser can be thrown on the diamonds if you can avoid losing three hearts early on, so the plan will be to set up diamonds and discard a heart. You should then make four spades, three diamonds and the ♣A.

The play: Play the ♡10 on the first trick. If South wins he will not wish to continue hearts and allow you to make the ♡K. You must be careful not to let North into the lead again to play another heart through dummy. If South switches to the ♣K let him hold the trick; you don't want your ♣A to be forced out and to lose a trick later to North's ♣Q or ♣J. Similarly, when you tackle the spades, play the ♠8 first; if North plays low you can play low in dummy. South may win with the doubleton ♠Q or ♠J but North is kept out of the lead. The diamond finesse, of course, will also be taken into the South hand.

Postscript: Assuming reasonable breaks, the contract should make on the defence described. A top class defender in the South seat might have defeated you by switching to a low club from a holding such as ♣K-Q-x-x at trick 2, as you could not then have kept North out of the lead.

♠ J 5 4	*Deal 53*. You are West. Your right-hand opponent
♡ A J 7 2	(South) opens 1♠, you pass, North passes and
◊ Q J 7 2	East (your partner) bids 2♠. South passes and it is
♣ Q J	up to you. What do you bid on this hand?

After 1♠-NB-NB your partner was in the protective position, where all bids are devalued. However, he has cue-bid the opponent's suit, one of the strongest courses of action he can take. You can expect him to have a shortage in the spade suit and good support for the other suits. That he has chosen to cue-bid rather than make a take-out double indicates that his hand is unsuitable for defending a spade contract and he is not giving you the opportunity to pass a double of 2♠ for penalties.

There are two possible bids that you should consider. Either 3♠, a return cue-bid as a strong forward-going manoeuvre, asking partner to choose the suit, or else a bid of your own major suit, hearts.

A game should be possible on this hand and if you bid hearts, it should be at least at game level.

The bidding	South	West	North	East
	1♠	NB	NB	2♠
	NB	4♡	All pass	

Although partner's hand (see below) is not strong enough for a cue-bid of the opponent's suit in second position, in the protective position it describes his hand quite well. Some players might have chosen a take-out double instead.

North leads the ◊3 against West's contract of 4♡. Plan the play.

♠ J 5 4		♠ Q
♡ A J 7 2	N	♡ K Q 10 4
◊ Q J 7 2	W E	◊ A 10 5 4
♣ Q J	S	♣ K 10 9 3

Planning: At first sight there appears to be only one club, one diamond and one spade loser (the clubs will provide discards for the other spades). But look carefully at that lead. It is the lowest diamond out; it's unlikely to be low from an honour as North would hardly underlead the ◊K when he could so easily lead his partner's suit. The ◊3 is, therefore, almost certainly a singleton, led in the hope of getting diamond ruffs.

The play: Go up with the ◊A. Draw trumps, hopefully in three rounds, and force out the ♣A. If the opponents switch to spades you can trump the second round in dummy and discard your last spade on a club before forcing out the ◊K.

Postscript: When this hand was first played declarer finessed the first diamond, losing to South's ◊K. A diamond came back, ruffed by North. Then a spade to South's ♠K and another diamond ruff. The ♣A from North was followed by the final insult, a second club from North, ruffed by South, who led his last diamond for North to ruff again. East-West were four down, and all because of the first round finesse.

♠ 5 3   *Deal 54.* You are West. Your right-hand opponent
♡ A J 9 5 2 (South) opens 1♡. What do you bid on this hand?
◊ J 7 2
♣ A J 7

If your opponent had opened 1♣ or 1◊ you would have considered an overcall of 1♡. However, when the opponents bid your best suit it is usually right to pass. True they may be 'psyching' by bidding a suit they have not got, but it is more likely that the bid is genuine and that the hand is a misfit. Left to themselves they are likely to get into a mess.

You pass and North passes. Your partner doubles and South passes. What do you do now?

Partner was in the protective position when he doubled but his action announces a fair hand, because a double is one of the strongest bids he can make. The fact that he doubled rather than making a cue-bid suggests that he probably doesn't have a void or singleton heart and that he is not completely averse to defending a heart contract.

With your powerful hearts, sitting over South's, and the balance of points your way, it seems most unlikely that South will make 1♡, and you should pass, converting your partner's take-out double into a penalty double.

The bidding	South	West	North	East
	1♡	NB	NB	Dbl
	NB	NB	NB	

Now it is up to you again. What do you lead? You don't wish to shorten your long trumps by ruffing side suits, so forget about leading a spade. A club or a diamond *could* work out well but might instead help declarer. Many players would avoid the lead of a trump up to South's strength but you have to face the fact that you will probably be thrown in later to lead trumps if you don't lead them now.

There is, therefore, a great deal to be said for a trump lead. If trumps are drawn and the hand is played as a no-trump contract, your side's greater power should crush declarer.

The full deal:

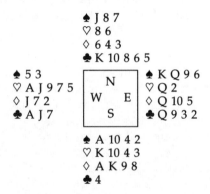

```
                    ♠ J 8 7
                    ♡ 8 6
                    ◊ 6 4 3
                    ♣ K 10 8 6 5
    ♠ 5 3                           ♠ K Q 9 6
    ♡ A J 9 7 5        N            ♡ Q 2
    ◊ J 7 2        W       E        ◊ Q 10 5
    ♣ A J 7            S            ♣ Q 9 3 2
                    ♠ A 10 4 2
                    ♡ K 10 4 3
                    ◊ A K 9 8
                    ♣ 4
```

Partner's ♡Q will draw declarer's ♡K so, when partner gains the lead and returns another trump, you will be able to clear the suit. Best defence will then make four trump tricks, a spade, a diamond and two clubs, limiting declarer to five tricks.

Postscript: If North had opened 1♡ and partner had doubled in second position, your hearts would not have been solid enough to pass the take-out double. However, it is a different story when you are sitting *over* declarer with a suit such as ♡A-J-9-7-5.

♠ Q 9 4   *Deal 55*. You are West. Your left-hand opponent
♡ A J 9 3   (North) opens 1◊ and the next two players pass.
◊ K 7 6   What do you bid on this hand?
♣ 7 6 2

Your partner may have had to pass on quite a respectable hand and it is up to you, in the protective position, to find a bid.

Probably 1♡ is the least unpleasant choice in this case as you are not strong enough to double, bid 1NT or cue-bid the opponent's suit. Over 1♡, North passes and your partner raises to 2♡.

The bidding	North	East	South	West
	1◊	NB	NB	1♡
	NB	2♡	All pass	

With a balanced 11 points (see below) your partner was not strong enough to bid on the first round. He raised your 1♡ to 2♡ to make sure that South didn't come in on the second round with belated support for diamonds or with a spade suit that he was too weak to bid first time.

Against West's contract of 2♡, North leads the ♣K-Q and continues with a third club to South's ♣A. South now returns the ◊9 to your ◊6, North's ◊8 and dummy's ◊Q. Plan the play.

♠ Q 9 4	N	♠ A J 5
♡ A J 9 3	W E	♡ K 6 5 4
◊ K 7 6	S	◊ Q 4 3
♣ 7 6 2		♣ J 5 4

Planning: South can have no high honour cards left, since he failed to respond to his partner's 1◊ bid and has already shown up with the ♣A. North, therefore, must have the ♠K, the ♡Q and presumably the ◊A-J sitting over your ◊K.

Your best chance is to throw North in, to lead a diamond up to your ◊K. You can manage this if North started with three clubs and five diamonds, a holding that looks quite possible from the bidding and play so far, as North will then have only five cards in the major suits.

The play: Don't finesse the ♡J (which could lose to North's ♡Q) but cash the ♡K and ♡A. If the ♡Q drops (i.e. North has two hearts and three spades), draw the last trump, then play a low spade to the ♠J, cash the ♠A and throw North in with the ♠K. If the ♡Q doesn't drop (i.e. North has three hearts and two spades), play a low spade to the ♠J, cash ♠A to drop North's ♠K and throw North in with the ♡Q. In either case North will have only diamonds left to lead and you will make your ◊K.

Postscript: This is not an easy hand to play but the bidding and play to the first few tricks give you much information about the North hand, so that you can avoid taking a losing heart finesse or playing the diamonds yourself.

CHAPTER 12

Opening Leads (The Principles)

The opening lead sets the tone for the whole defence. Success or failure of the contract often depends on what lead is made and it is essential to get it right. Unfortunately opening leads are the very worst department of many players' game, so it is worth spending a little time on the strategy that should guide you in selecting this vital card.

Basically there are two sorts of opening lead, the attacking lead and the passive lead. An attacking lead is an attempt to set up a trick (or tricks) for your side. For example, you might lead a low heart from ♡A-Q-10-x-x against a no-trump contract, hoping to force out the other honours and to make several heart tricks later. Or with the ♠A and ♡K-Q-x you would lead the ♡K to force out the ♡A against a contract of 6♠, so that when you won the lead with the ♠A you would have the ♡Q to cash.

In contrast, the passive lead is an attempt not to give a trick away. For example, if the opponents bid 1♠-4♠ and you hold ♠8-6-3, the lead of a spade is unlikely to help opponents. Trumps may be distributed something like this:

♠ K x x x		♠ K x x x
♠ 8 6 3	♠ x x	or	♠ 8 6 3	♠ Q x
♠ A Q x x		♠ A J 10 x

In the first example opponents have no loser in trumps; in the second, you will help them find the ♠Q but they could have done that for themselves anyway.

To see why players often choose a passive rather than an

attacking lead, consider the following situation:

$$\clubsuit K 8 4 3$$
$$\clubsuit Q 7 2 \qquad \clubsuit A 9 5$$
$$\clubsuit J 10 6$$

If either West or East leads the suit, their side will take only one trick and North-South will make three tricks. However, if either North or South leads the suit, they will make only two tricks and East-West will make two. Get out the cards and try it for yourself and you will see that whoever leads the suit gives away a trick. Similarly with Q-x-x oppposite J-x-x, or with K-x-x opposite J-x-x, if opponents lead the suit you only have to play low second in hand to be reasonably sure of making a trick, but if you lead the suit yourself you can easily lose all three tricks. Thus, if you lead from a suit that has an unsupported honour, or from a 'tenace' such as K-J-x or A-Q-x or from two touching honours such as K-Q-x, you are quite likely to give a trick to the opponents. It may still be the right lead if it is necessary to set up a trick for your side quickly before opponents can throw their losers away.

The general strategy you should adopt, therefore, is to try to find an attacking lead if the opponents are in a high level contract and the bidding has indicated that they have long suits on which they will be able to discard their losers. However, if the opponents are in a low-level contract and particularly if they have shown rather balanced hands, you should aim for a safe, passive lead that won't give a trick away.

Some conventions in leading

If you decide to lead a suit of three or more cards headed by an honour you should lead a low card (low from an honour) but try to avoid this lead if you can. If you lead a suit that has no high cards, for example 7-5-2, it is conventional to lead the 'top of nothing', the 7. Alternatively, you can agree with your partner to play MUD (middle-up-down) against suit contracts, in which case you would lead the 5, play the 7 on the next round and then the 2. Some players use MUD leads against no-trump contracts also despite possible confusion with fourth highest leads (see p.143).

If partner leads and you are third player

It is often said that third player should play high. He should, however, play only as high as is necessary to win the trick. Thus, if partner leads the ◇8 ('top of nothing') and dummy plays low from ◇K-6-2, you should play the ◇J from ◇A-Q-J-2 so that when the ◇J holds the trick your partner will deduce that you have the ◇A-Q as well. Similarly, if partner leads the ♠2 (low from an honour) and dummy plays low from ♠K-6-3, you should play the ♠10 from ♠A-J-10-4.

If you can't win the trick, that is if your partner leads (or dummy plays) a card higher than any you hold, you can indicate whether you would like partner to lead the suit again by playing the highest card you can spare, to encourage continuation of the suit, or a low card to discourage. We have already seen how useful these signals can be to the defence, on Deal 41, and will encounter them again (Chapter 15).

♠ 6 4 3	*Deal 56.* You are West and hold this hand. Your
♡ K 9 6 4	right-hand opponent (South) opens 1♠, North
◇ K 10 7	raises to 3♠ and South bids 4♠. What is your
♣ A 10 2	opening lead?

Ask yourself the question, what has the bidding told you? South has shown spades and a more-than-minimum hand; North has shown spade support and about 10-12 points. Neither has given any indication that he has an unbalanced hand with long side suits that could provide discards.

Looking at the choices open to you, a club lead is most unattractive; you should not underlead an ace against a suit contract and to lead the ♣A may simply set up the opponents' ♣K. A lead away from either red suit king might enable declarer to make a queen that he could not otherwise make or might kill what little strength your partner holds. The only safe lead is a trump, after which you can let declarer make all the going himself. In this case a simple process of elimination led you to a trump lead.

♠ A J 8 7
♡ 5 2
◊ A J 4
♣ 9 8 7 4

♠ 6 4 3
♡ K 9 6 4
◊ K 10 7
♣ A 10 2

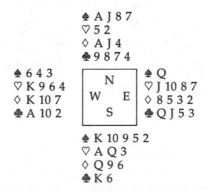

You lead the ♣3. Partner's ♠Q falls to South's ♠K and two more rounds of trumps are drawn, partner discarding the ◊2 and ◊3. The ♡2 is now led from dummy to declarer's ♡Q and your ♡K. What do you lead now?

With no more trumps left, should you now switch to a club or a diamond? The answer is no. The reasons that put you off these leads before still apply and you should continue with your passive defence. You have already made your heart trick and this is now the only suit in which you can't give anything away, so exit with a heart and let declarer struggle on.

The full deal:

♠ A J 8 7
♡ 5 2
◊ A J 4
♣ 9 8 7 4

♠ 6 4 3   ♠ Q
♡ K 9 6 4   ♡ J 10 8 7
◊ K 10 7   ◊ 8 5 3 2
♣ A 10 2   ♣ Q J 5 3

♠ K 10 9 5 2
♡ A Q 3
◊ Q 9 6
♣ K 6

The spade opening lead cost the defence nothing as the ♠Q would have dropped anyway. The heart return also doesn't help declarer. With this defence, declarer can make only five spades, the ♡A, a heart ruff and two diamonds. He will have to lose one heart trick, one diamond and two clubs if he has to open up the suit himself.

Postscript: The passive defence consists of finding a safe lead and getting off lead safely each time you take a trick (usually by returning the suit in which you have just won a trick). If West opens up the hearts, diamonds or clubs he will present declarer with a tenth trick.

Even against good defence an astute declarer can make his contract by drawing trumps, ending in his own hand, finessing the ◊J, cashing the ◊A and throwing West in with the ◊K, to open up the hearts or clubs. This throw-in technique is similar to that described on the previous deal.

♠ 6 2
♡ J 7 5 2
◊ 9 8 6
♣ K J 9 2

Deal 57. You are West. South opens 1♠ and the bidding goes:

South	North
1♠	2◊
3◊	3♠
4♠	

What is your opening lead?

What has the bidding told you? The opponents have a fit in spades (probably South has five, and North three) and a fit in diamonds. Left to himself, declarer will probably draw trumps, run the diamonds and discard a losing heart or club from his own hand. You must attack quickly to make your winners before South gets a discard. An attacking lead is called for, and a heart or a club must be led, despite the holding of an unsupported honour in hearts and a tenace in clubs. Avoid the clubs, which are altogether too dangerous, and lead the ♡2. Dummy goes down:

♠ Q 9 4
♡ 8 4 3
◊ A K 7 5 3
♣ 6 4

♠ 6 2
♡ J 7 5 2
◊ 9 8 6
♣ K J 9 2

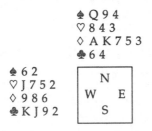

Partner wins the first trick with the ♡K and switches to ♣A. Declarer plays the ♣5. What do you play? You can't take the club trick but you *can* signal to partner whether or not you want the club suit continued. The ♣2 would indicate that you did not want him to lead another club; the ♣9 (the highest card that you can spare) encourages him to lead the suit again, and when he does, your ♣K makes. You now lead a heart to partner's ♡A, which is the fourth trick for the defence.

The full deal:

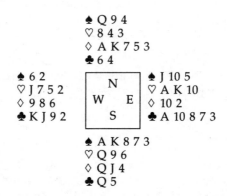

```
                    ♠ Q 9 4
                    ♡ 8 4 3
                    ◊ A K 7 5 3
                    ♣ 6 4
    ♠ 6 2                          ♠ J 10 5
    ♡ J 7 5 2         N            ♡ A K 10
    ◊ 9 8 6       W       E        ◊ 10 2
    ♣ K J 9 2         S            ♣ A 10 8 7 3
                    ♠ A K 8 7 3
                    ♡ Q 9 6
                    ◊ Q J 4
                    ♣ Q 5
```

On the passive lead of a trump (or a diamond) declarer would have made five spade tricks and five diamonds, discarding a losing heart or club, thus restricting his losers to three. Because of the danger of discards the defence must attack and take its tricks early.

♠ 10 8   *Deal 58.* You are West. South opens 1♡, North
♡ J 9 7 2   responds 1NT and South rebids 2♡. What is your
◊ K Q J 9 2   opening lead?
♣ 10 7

There are two reasons for leading the ◊K. First, you have a sequence and 'top of a sequence' is one of the best leads in the game. It has the advantage of being attacking (to set up tricks for your side) and at the same time safe, for a sequence lead can hardly give tricks away.

The full deal:

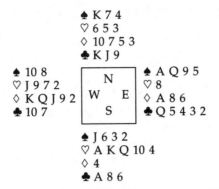

```
                    ♠ K 7 4
                    ♡ 6 5 3
                    ◇ 10 7 5 3
                    ♣ K J 9
    ♠ 10 8              ┌─────┐         ♠ A Q 9 5
    ♡ J 9 7 2           │  N  │         ♡ 8
    ◇ K Q J 9 2      W  │     │  E      ◇ A 8 6
    ♣ 10 7              │  S  │         ♣ Q 5 4 3 2
                        └─────┘
                    ♠ J 6 3 2
                    ♡ A K Q 10 4
                    ◇ 4
                    ♣ A 8 6
```

The second reason for leading a diamond is that you have four trumps. With such a trump holding it's best to lead your own long suit and force declarer to ruff. You may finish up with more trumps than he has and so take control of the hand.

On the lead of the ◇K, your partner will play the ◇8, to encourage. You will continue with a low diamond and declarer will trump your partner's ◇A. Declarer will try to draw trumps, will discover the bad break and may now switch to a black suit. If partner gains the lead, he will lead another diamond to force declarer to trump again. Now you will have more trumps than declarer and will hope to gain the lead with your last trump and still have some diamonds to cash. Declarer may try to turn the tables on you by playing on black suits to make you ruff and shorten your trumps, so the hand is likely to develop into a cat and mouse game.

Postscript: The lead is easy to find on this hand as the diamond sequence is so attractive. However, even with a weaker 5-card diamond suit West should still lead a diamond to force declarer, as before. It is a mistake, with four or more reasonably good trumps, to lead a short suit in the hope of getting ruffs because, if you ruff, you give up natural trump tricks. Consider the effect of a short suit lead on the hand we've been talking about. A spade will help declarer to establish a spade trick and a club lead will kill partner's ♣Q.

♠ A 5
♡ A 6 5
◇ 10 9 8 2
♣ 10 9 7 2

Deal 59. You are West. South opens 1♠ and the bidding goes:

	South	North
	1♠	2♣
	2♡	NB

What is your opening lead?

The bidding is curious, so what have the opponents got? Obviously North was keen to drop the bidding early so he is not strong. Why did he not return to his partner's first suit when South may well have more spades than hearts? The reason must be that North is very short of spades (a singleton or void perhaps) but has at least a semi-fit for hearts. Declarer's plan will be to lead spades from his own hand and ruff them in dummy. Now that you've worked that out it's up to you to thwart him. Lead a trump at every opportunity to prevent dummy from ruffing spades.

The only question that remains is which trump to lead. If you had only the doubleton ♡A-x it would be correct to lead the ♡A and then the low one. With ♡A-x-x lead low, hoping to regain the lead before declarer starts his ruffing, and then lead ♡A and your third trump, removing *three* potential ruffing cards from dummy.

The full deal:

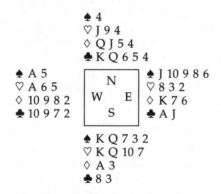

```
                    ♠ 4
                    ♡ J 9 4
                    ◇ Q J 5 4
                    ♣ K Q 6 5 4
  ♠ A 5                          ♠ J 10 9 8 6
  ♡ A 6 5          N             ♡ 8 3 2
  ◇ 10 9 8 2    W     E          ◇ K 7 6
  ♣ 10 9 7 2       S             ♣ A J
                    ♠ K Q 7 3 2
                    ♡ K Q 10 7
                    ◇ A 3
                    ♣ 8 3
```

You lead the ♡5. When you regain the lead with the ♠A, you lead ♡A and another heart to remove all dummy's trumps. Denied any spade ruffs, declarer can't make eight tricks.

Postscript: Again the bidding told you what to lead. When the opponents play in their secondary suit, as they did on this hand, a trump lead is almost always best.

♠ 8 7 6
♡ Q 3
◇ K 7 3
♣ A Q 10 6 2

Deal 60. You are West and hold this hand. What do you lead against each of the bidding sequences shown below?

(a) *South*	*North*	(b) *South*	*North*	(c) *East*	*South*	*West*	*North*
1NT	2NT	1♠	2♣	1◇	1♡	2♣	3♡
3NT		NB		All pass			

(a) With a good 5-card suit and a possible outside entry, it usually pays to attack against a no-trump contract. By leading a club you may give away a trick but you hope to get it back later, with interest. It is conventional to lead the fourth highest (fourth from the top) so the ♣6 is correct.

(b) There is no point in setting up your long suit on this hand as your low clubs will be trumped. The opponents are in a low level contract and, although their spades will be strong, there is no indication that they have long suits, on which losers can be discarded. A passive lead is called for, and the only passive lead you have on this hand is a trump.

(c) This time partner has called so the opening lead is easy – you lead his suit. A low diamond please, not the ◇K. After all, the diamonds may be distributed thus:

$$◇ x x x$$
◇ K x x   ◇ A J 10 x
$$◇ Q x x$$

If you make the mistake of leading the ◇K, declarer's ◇Q will always make a trick. If you lead a low diamond, partner can win with his ◇A and lead back his ◇J to trap the ◇Q and ensure three diamond tricks for the defence.

Even if the diamonds are distributed differently:

$$◇ Q x x$$
◇ K x x   ◇ A J 10 x
$$◇ x x x$$

the lead of a low diamond from West is still correct; partner can win the first trick cheaply with the ◊10 and the defence still have the ◊A and ◊K left to crush the ◊Q.

Postscript: On the same hand, therefore, one could make many different leads, depending on the bidding. Listen carefully to the opponents' bidding and try to build up a picture of their hands. Decide on whether to make a passive or an attacking lead; this will point you to the right suit, and the choice of the right card in that suit is a matter of convention.

CHAPTER 13

Leads Against No-trump Contracts

Top of a sequence

If you attack in your long suit against opponents' no-trump contract and are lucky enough to have a sequence of three or more touching cards, the lead of the top of a sequence is best. Thus from the following holdings you should lead the card underlined.

- (a) <u>K</u>QJ72
- (b) <u>Q</u>J1084
- (c) <u>J</u>10963
- (d) K<u>J</u>1095
- (e) AQ<u>J</u>104

Don't lead the fourth best from such combinations. For example in (b) you could easily give away a trick if declarer held A-9-x facing K-x-x. Leads (d) and (e) are top of an internal sequence, sound practice against no-trumps but not against suit contracts.

Your suit or partner's suit?

There is not much point in setting up your own long suit if you have no entries. If you think your partner has more entries than you have, it will often pay to try to set up his long suit instead of yours. You may have to guess what this suit is, but the opponents' bidding will guide you.

The double of 3NT

The double of 3NT is basically for penalties, and the time to double is when you think the opponents have bid their hands to the limit and you can see that the cards lie badly for them. However, when the double is made by a player whose partner is about to make the opening lead, it usually has a lead-directing function too.

So if your partner doubles the opponents' 3NT contract and you are about to make the opening lead, you should be guided by the following principles:

1 If *you* have bid a suit, he is asking you to lead it. He probably has some undisclosed support for it.
2 If your partner has called a suit, he is asking you to lead it, and not to be put off by the opponents calling no-trumps over it.
3 If the opponents have bid suits but your side has not, he is asking you to lead dummy's suit.
4 If neither side has bid suits (e.g. 1NT-3NT) and his double comes 'out of the blue', he has a solid suit, probably a major, that he wants you to lead.

♠ 9 5   *Deal 61*. You are West. Your right-hand opponent
♡ K 7 6 5   (South) opens 1NT and North raises him to 3NT.
◇ 8 5 4   What is your opening lead from this hand?
♣ 9 8 3 2

Some players would automatically lead their long suit against this no-trump contract but there is not much chance of defeating the opponents on a heart lead. Your poor suit is unlikely to pose much of a threat to declarer and, even if you could establish some heart winners, you have no outside entries with which to gain the lead. You have only 3 points so the balance of the defensive strength must lie with your partner. You must try to guess what partner's suit is and lead that. It is slightly more likely that partner has a good major suit than a minor as, if the opponents had strength in a major, they might well be playing in that suit, instead of in no-trumps. So your lead is the ♠9, the top card of your doubleton.

The full deal:

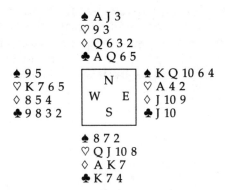

```
                    ♠ A J 3
                    ♡ 9 3
                    ◇ Q 6 3 2
                    ♣ A Q 6 5
     ♠ 9 5                          ♠ K Q 10 6 4
     ♡ K 7 6 5        N             ♡ A 4 2
     ◇ 8 5 4      W       E         ◇ J 10 9
     ♣ 9 8 3 2        S             ♣ J 10
                    ♠ 8 7 2
                    ♡ Q J 10 8
                    ◇ A K 7
                    ♣ K 7 4
```

If dummy plays low on the first trick, your partner will play a higher than necessary spade, the ♠6, to encourage you to continue with the spades. The ♠A will then be forced out early and, although declarer can make one spade trick and seven tricks in the minor suits, he will have to tackle the hearts eventually. Partner will then gain the lead and cash his winning spades, to defeat the contract.

Postscript: A heart lead would have removed partner's entry and declarer would have made the contract by playing on hearts for extra tricks. The defence can beat the contract on any lead other than a low heart provided that, when hearts are played, West goes up with his ♡K and switches to a spade. The defence is similar to that on Deal 43.

♠ 9 8 3 2	*Deal 62.* You are West and hold this hand. Your
♡ 8 4	right-hand opponent (South) opens 1NT and the
◇ A 7 5 3	bidding goes:
♣ 8 7 5	

	South	North
	1NT	2♣
	2◇	3NT

What is your opening lead?

This is another hand where partner has most of the defensive strength so you must try to find his suit. The bidding has been very informative. North must have four cards in one or both majors to make the Stayman 2♣ enquiry but he probably does not have a

5-card major as he could have bid it over 2◊. South has denied a 4-card major by his 2◊ bid. The opponents can't have more than seven cards between them in either major suit and, as you have only two hearts, it follows that your partner must have at least four, maybe five. The ♡8, therefore, is your lead; you will lead the ♡4 later if you get the chance and if East has shown interest in your choice.

The full deal:

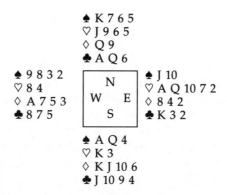

```
                    ♠ K 7 6 5
                    ♡ J 9 6 5
                    ◊ Q 9
                    ♣ A Q 6
    ♠ 9 8 3 2           N          ♠ J 10
    ♡ 8 4                           ♡ A Q 10 7 2
    ◊ A 7 5 3      W        E      ◊ 8 4 2
    ♣ 8 7 5            S           ♣ K 3 2
                    ♠ A Q 4
                    ♡ K 3
                    ◊ K J 10 6
                    ♣ J 10 9 4
```

The heart lead gets the defence off on the right foot. If North plays low, East will encourage with the ♡7. If North covers the ♡8 with the ♡9 or ♡J, East will cover with a higher card to force out declarer's ♡K. West continues hearts when he gets in with the ◊A, to defeat the contract.

♠ 8 5 4
♡ 10 5 4 2
◊ A 5 4
♣ 8 7 4

Deal 63. You are East and you hold this hand. Your left-hand opponent (South) opens 1NT and North bids 3NT. Your partner leads the ◊J and the dummy goes down.

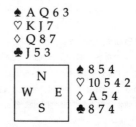

```
                    ♠ A Q 6 3
                    ♡ K J 7
                    ◊ Q 8 7
                    ♣ J 5 3
                        N          ♠ 8 5 4
                                   ♡ 10 5 4 2
                    W        E    ◊ A 5 4
                        S          ♣ 8 7 4
```

Contract 3NT by South. Partner (West) leads the ◊J, and dummy plays the ◊7. Which card do you play?

Partner knows that he has more defensive values than you and he is likely to have led *his* best suit. The lead could be from ◊J-10-9-x-(x) or ◊K-J-10-9-(x). If the former, you can't prevent declarer from making his ◊K and it would be wrong to play the ◊A for he would then make both ◊K and ◊Q. If the latter, you still must not play the ◊A because partner's ◊J will hold the trick and he can continue with another diamond to trap the ◊Q. So you must save your ◊A but do your best to encourage your partner to continue the suit by playing the ◊5, the highest you can afford.

The full deal:

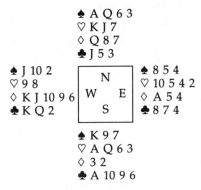

```
              ♠ A Q 6 3
              ♡ K J 7
              ◊ Q 8 7
              ♣ J 5 3
♠ J 10 2                      ♠ 8 5 4
♡ 9 8          N              ♡ 10 5 4 2
◊ K J 10 9 6  W   E           ◊ A 5 4
♣ K Q 2          S            ♣ 8 7 4
              ♠ K 9 7
              ♡ A Q 6 3
              ◊ 3 2
              ♣ A 10 9 6
```

The lead of the ◊J is the most effective defence. If it holds the trick partner will continue with the ◊10. Now you *must* play the ◊A to unblock the suit, whether or not dummy's ◊Q is played. Then your last diamond back will give the defence five tricks.

Postscript: The hold-up of your high diamond on the first round to threaten the high card in dummy is known as 'finessing against dummy', a standard defensive play.

♠ 10 9 8   *Deal 64*. You are East and hold this hand. Your
♡ 10 7 6 4 3   left-hand opponent (South) opens 1NT and the
◊ 10 5   bidding goes: *South*   *North*
♣ A 6 2   1NT   2♣
                                 2♠   3NT

Your partner leads the ♣J and dummy goes down:

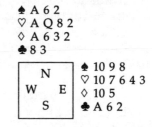

```
          ♠ A 6 2
          ♡ A Q 8 2
          ◊ A 6 3 2
          ♣ 8 3
     ┌─────────┐   ♠ 10 9 8
     │    N    │   ♡ 10 7 6 4 3
     │  W   E  │   ◊ 10 5
     │    S    │   ♣ A 6 2
     └─────────┘
```

Dummy's ♣3 is played on partner's lead of the ♣J. Which card do you play?

Ask yourself the question, who has the ♣Q? Certainly not partner, for with the ♣Q and ♣J he would have led the ♣Q. You must play the ♣A to prevent declarer winning with the ♣Q and then return the ♣6, not the ♣2, to help partner to count the suit (p.97).

The full deal:

```
              ♠ A 6 2
              ♡ A Q 8 2
              ◊ A 6 3 2
              ♣ 8 3
  ♠ 5 4 3    ┌─────────┐   ♠ 10 9 8
  ♡ 9 5      │    N    │   ♡ 10 7 6 4 3
  ◊ K Q 4    │  W   E  │   ◊ 10 5
  ♣ K J 10 9 7│   S    │   ♣ A 6 2
             └─────────┘
              ♠ K Q J 7
              ♡ K J
              ◊ J 9 8 7
              ♣ Q 5 4
```

The defence should make the first five club tricks. To fail to play the ♣A in this situation is to 'finesse against partner', a play that makes you most unpopular. True, partner may have led from ♣J-10-9-x-(x) leaving declarer with ♣K-Q-x-(x) but, if so, declarer will make two club tricks whether you play the ♣A on the first round or not. The play of the ♣A gives the best chance of defeating the contract; in contrast to the last hand there is no high card in dummy for which to save it.

♠ 8 7 4 3
♡ 8 3
♢ K J 8 6 5
♣ 10 7

Deal 65. You are West and hold this hand. Your left-hand opponent (North) opens 1♠ and the bidding goes:

North	East	South	West
1♠	NB	2♣	NB
2♡	NB	2NT	NB
3NT	Dbl	All pass	

What is your opening lead?

Doubles of 3NT are for penalties but are also lead-directing. In this instance, as neither defender has bid a suit, your partner is asking you to lead dummy's suit. Dummy has bid two suits, so you must decide which. You hold four spades yourself, and you know dummy has at least four so it's unlikely that partner has much length in this suit. It is much more likely that he wants a heart lead, as your shortage in hearts indicates that partner may have length. So you lead the ♡8.

The full deal:

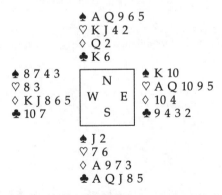

```
              ♠ A Q 9 6 5
              ♡ K J 4 2
              ♢ Q 2
              ♣ K 6
♠ 8 7 4 3          N          ♠ K 10
♡ 8 3                         ♡ A Q 10 9 5
♢ K J 8 6 5   W     E         ♢ 10 4
♣ 10 7             S          ♣ 9 4 3 2
              ♠ J 2
              ♡ 7 6
              ♢ A 9 7 3
              ♣ A Q J 8 5
```

Dummy plays low and, although your partner would like to encourage, he has to play the ♡5 to keep you on lead. When your ♡8 holds the trick it is obvious that you must continue with hearts. Partner will win the second trick and play the ♡A and another to clear the suit whilst he still has the ♠K as an entry, and the defence will take five tricks.

CHAPTER 14

Doubles

We have, by now, met three different types of double and it should be useful to summarise them here.

The take-out double

This is a bidding device to force partner to show his best suit. It occurs at a low level of bidding when partner has not so far bid.

North	East	South	West		North	East	South	West
1♣	Dbl				1◇	NB	NB	Dbl

North	East	South	West		North	East	South	West
1◇	NB	2◇	Dbl		1◇	NB	1♡	Dbl

In the last example West is asking his partner to choose between the two unbid (black) suits.

The penalty double (business double)

Penalty doubles are made when you think the opponents can't make their contract, to increase the penalties they suffer. Penalty doubles include the double of:

1   1NT opening bids;
2   Overcalls. The double cannot be for take-out because partner has bid;
3   Contracts reached after a competitive auction;

4   Most game or slam contracts, particularly when the doubler is
     on lead, so the double cannot be to direct a lead (see below).

Lead-directing doubles

The lead-directing implications of a double of 3NT have already
been discussed (p.136). In addition, the double of a slam contract
by a player whose partner is to make the opening lead also has a
lead-directing function. It is named, after its inventor, the Lightner
slam double. The theory behind this convention is that, if the
opponents have overbid their hands, they will get a bad result
anyway and a penalty double will not increase the penalties much.
The double, therefore, can be more profitably used to indicate a
special lead, usually a suit in which the doubler is void, so as to
defeat a soundly bid slam that would otherwise make.

Fourth highest leads and the 'rule of eleven'

When you lead a long suit against a no-trump contract and you
don't have a sequence, it is conventional to lead the fourth highest
card (the fourth from the top, e.g. K-8-6-4-3). By looking at his own
hand, at dummy and at the card led, the other defender can work
out how many cards declarer holds that are higher than the card
led. He does this by applying the 'rule of eleven'.

To see how this rule works, imagine that the player on lead holds
A-K-Q-J in his suit. Of course, it would be wrong for him to lead
the fourth best from this holding, but suppose it amuses him to
lead his jack. There is no card in the other three hands that will beat
it. If from A-K-Q-10 he (wrongly) leads the 10, there will be one
card in the other three hands higher than the card led and so on:

Card led	No of cards in the other three hands higher than the card led
J	0
10	1
9	2
8	3
7	4 etc

The jack (the eleventh card in the sense that it is the card above the ten) is the baseline for fourth highest leads. By subtracting the number of the card led from eleven, you learn the number of cards in the other three hands that are higher than the card led.

For example:

$$\diamond K 6 3$$

$$\diamond A J 7 4 2 \qquad\qquad \diamond 8 5$$

$$\diamond Q 10 9$$

When West leads the $\diamond$4 and dummy goes down, East applies the 'rule of eleven'. Four from eleven equals seven. There are, therefore, seven cards in the other three hands that will beat the card led. As he can see four of them in his own hand and dummy, he knows declarer has three cards higher than the four. Similarly declarer can work out that East has two cards higher than the four. Although the lead gives information to the declarer, it often helps the defence more, in knowing whether to continue with the suit. It is helpful also to know that when partner leads the 2 (or leads the 3 and you can see the 2 in dummy or your own hand) he has only a 4-card suit, as he can't have a lower card.

♠ 3
♡ A 7 5 3
◇ K 9 6 3
♣ K 10 8 2

Deal 66. You are West and hold this hand. Your partner (East) bids 1♠ and your right-hand opponent (South) overcalls with 2♡. What do you bid now?

The hand is a misfit. You have only a singleton in your partner's suit but a 4-card holding in the opponents' suit. There is an old bridge adage which says, 'Let the opponents play the misfits… we'll play the fits'. Your side holds the balance of points and the cards lie badly for the opponents, so they are unlikely to make their contract, and you should double. Partner will recognise that your double of an overcall is for penalties and, unless his hand is very unsuitable for defence, he will pass. Assuming that your double is passed out, what do you lead?

Although you hold the ♡A your other trumps are low, and the best use you can make of them is to ruff spades. So you lead the singleton of your partner's suit and dummy goes down:

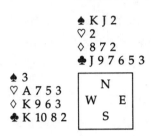

```
        ♠ K J 2
        ♡ 2
        ◊ 8 7 2
        ♣ J 9 7 6 5 3
♠ 3
♡ A 7 5 3        N
◊ K 9 6 3    W       E
♣ K 10 8 2       S
```

Your spade lead is taken by dummy's ♠K and dummy's ♡2 is led to declarer's ♡Q. Plan the defence.

It appears that partner lacks the ace, king and jack of his suit, so his strength must lie elsewhere. To obtain spade ruffs you must try to put him on lead with the minor suits. Win with the ♡A and try to give partner the lead by underleading one of your kings. If this succeeds and you get a spade ruff, underlead your other king to put partner on lead again to give you another spade ruff.

The full deal:

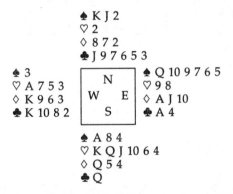

```
              ♠ K J 2
              ♡ 2
              ◊ 8 7 2
              ♣ J 9 7 6 5 3
♠ 3                        ♠ Q 10 9 7 6 5
♡ A 7 5 3      N           ♡ 9 8
◊ K 9 6 3   W     E        ◊ A J 10
♣ K 10 8 2     S           ♣ A 4
              ♠ A 8 4
              ♡ K Q J 10 6 4
              ◊ Q 5 4
              ♣ Q
```

After losing the first spade trick the defence wins the ♡A, the ◊3 to the ◊A, a spade ruff, the ♣2 to the ♣A (dropping South's ♣Q) and a second spade ruff. West now gets off lead with a heart and the defence must take another two diamond tricks later, putting the contract two down.

Postscript: This is the type of double many players will miss. For a successful low-level penalty double the doubler needs (a) a dislike of partner's suit, (b) a liking for the opponent's suit and (c) general

♠ 3
♡ 9 7 6 3
◊ K Q J 10 5
♣ Q 4 3

Deal 67. You are West and hold this hand. Your left-hand opponent (North) opens 2♡, a forcing bid showing a hand of 8 or more playing tricks. South responds 3♠, a jump bid in a forcing situation, showing a completely solid suit. North raises to 7♠ and your partner doubles.

The bidding	North	East	South	West
	2♡	NB	3♠	NB
	7♠	Dbl	All pass	

What is your opening lead?

Without the double you would have led the ◊K, a safe but attacking lead from the top of your sequence. However, partner's is a Lightner slam double calling for an unusual lead. The opponents are hardly likely to lose a trick to an ace, but with such distributional hands around the table it is quite possible that partner has a void. North has a long heart suit for his opening bid and you have four hearts, so it looks as if partner's shortage is in that suit. So lead a heart; on this hand it does not matter which one.

The full deal:

```
              ♠ 9 8 7 5
              ♡ A K Q J 10 8
              ◊ –
              ♣ A K 2
♠ 3                          ♠ 6 2
♡ 9 7 6 3         N          ♡ –
◊ K Q J 10 5   W     E       ◊ A 8 7 6 4 3 2
♣ Q 4 3           S          ♣ J 10 6 5
              ♠ A K Q J 10 4
              ♡ 5 4 2
              ◊ 9
              ♣ 9 8 7
```

On any other lead declarer can make his contract with ease but the heart lead is ruffed at trick one. Particularly unfortunate for North-South when 7♡ is impregnable!

♠ Q 10 8 6 2   *Deal 68*. You are West and hold this hand. Your
♡ K 9 4   right-hand opponent (South) opens 2NT and
◇ Q J 9   North raises him to 3NT. What is your opening
♣ 10 6   lead?

It is clear that you hold most of the defensive strength so you should lead your own suit. The fourth highest card of your longest suit is conventional, so the ♠6 is correct. Dummy goes down:

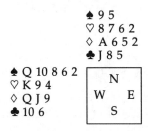

                      ♠ 9 5
                      ♡ 8 7 6 2
                      ◇ A 6 5 2
                      ♣ J 8 5

♠ Q 10 8 6 2
♡ K 9 4
◇ Q J 9
♣ 10 6

Dummy's hand is fairly minimum for his raise, so declarer will have to work for his contract. On your spade lead, dummy plays the ♠5, partner wins with the ♠A and declarer plays the ♠4. Partner now returns the ♠3, declarer plays the ♠7 and you win with the ♠10. What do you play now?

You must resist the temptation to play another spade. Partner returned his lowest spade so he must have had two or four of them (p.97). He can't have started with ♠A-K-J-3 or he would have played ♠K, ♠A, ♠J, then ♠3 to clear the suit. Partner must, therefore, have had ♠A-3 and declarer ♠K-J-7-4. If you lead the suit again you will give declarer two spade tricks. You must switch to another suit; the ◇Q 'through strength to weakness' looks the safest bet.

The full deal:

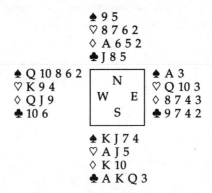

```
                    ♠ 9 5
                    ♡ 8 7 6 2
                    ◊ A 6 5 2
                    ♣ J 8 5
     ♠ Q 10 8 6 2    ┌─────────┐    ♠ A 3
     ♡ K 9 4         │    N    │    ♡ Q 10 3
     ◊ Q J 9         │ W     E │    ◊ 8 7 4 3
     ♣ 10 6          │    S    │    ♣ 9 7 4 2
                    └─────────┘
                    ♠ K J 7 4
                    ♡ A J 5
                    ◊ K 10
                    ♣ A K Q 3
```

Left to himself, declarer can make only eight tricks; a careless continuation of the spade suit would have given him his ninth.

Postscript: It is impossible to play a tight defence unless defenders follow established conventions in leading and in returning the correct card of partner's suit.

♠ 7 5 2   *Deal 69.* You are East and hold this hand. Your
♡ K 7   left-hand opponent (South) opens 1NT (12-14
◊ Q 10 9 8 points) and North raises to 3NT. West (your
♣ K J 8 3   partner) leads the ♡3 and dummy goes down:

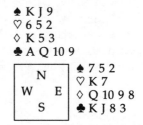

```
          ♠ K J 9
          ♡ 6 5 2
          ◊ K 5 3
          ♣ A Q 10 9
       ┌─────────┐  ♠ 7 5 2
       │    N    │  ♡ K 7
       │ W     E │  ◊ Q 10 9 8
       │    S    │  ♣ K J 8 3
       └─────────┘
```

Dummy plays ♡2, you play ♡K, and South plays ♡4. What do you return?

If partner has led his fourth highest, he can have only four hearts; he can't have a fifth card below the ♡3 as you can see the ♡2 in dummy. Declarer must also have four hearts. Look at it from the point of view of the 'rule of eleven'. Three from eleven = eight cards in the other three hands that can beat the card led. There are two such cards in dummy, two in your hand, so declarer must have started with four cards higher than the ♡3. If you continue hearts you will set up tricks for declarer, so you must switch to something else. A diamond looks best, so lead the ◊10, the top of your internal sequence.

The full deal:

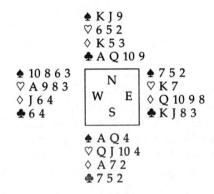

```
                    ♠ K J 9
                    ♡ 6 5 2
                    ◊ K 5 3
                    ♣ A Q 10 9
    ♠ 10 8 6 3          N          ♠ 7 5 2
    ♡ A 9 8 3                      ♡ K 7
    ◊ J 6 4         W     E        ◊ Q 10 9 8
    ♣ 6 4              S           ♣ K J 8 3
                    ♠ A Q 4
                    ♡ Q J 10 4
                    ◊ A 7 2
                    ♣ 7 5 2
```

If declarer plays the ◊A on your diamond return, your partner will encourage with the ◊6. East-West have merely to continue with diamonds each time they gain the lead, to defeat the contract. If the defence had repeatedly persisted with hearts, declarer would have had time to set up nine tricks.

♠ 6 5 2   *Deal 70.* You are East and hold this hand. Your
♡ 9 7 6   left-hand opponent (South) opens the bidding
◊ K 8 7   with 1♡ and the bidding goes:

♣ K J 4 2

South	North
1♡	2♣
3NT	NB

Your partner (West) leads the ♠J and dummy goes down:

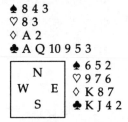

Declarer wins the spade lead with ♠Q and leads the ♣6 to West's ♣8, dummy's ♣9 and your ♣J. What do you lead now?

It is tempting to continue spades to set up partner's suit but there is much more urgent work to be done. Declarer can probably make his contract only if he can establish the clubs, so you must take the entry out of dummy. You must lead the ◊K (a low diamond will not do), and if that is ducked, continue with another diamond to force out the ◊A whilst you still have control of the clubs. This entry-killing play is known as the Merrimac Coup.

The full deal:

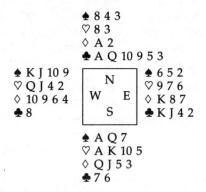

With the ◊A gone, declarer can make only two spades, two hearts, three diamonds and one club trick. The switch to diamonds by the defence gives up a diamond trick but saves several tricks in clubs.

CHAPTER 15

Signals

When you play to a trick in defence, your main aim will be to win the trick with the lowest card necessary. When you can't win the trick you will have a choice of cards to play and you can use these to pass a message to your partner.

Thus, when partner leads a suit, the play of a high card encourages him to continue the suit and a low card discourages, suggesting that he switches to something else. Similarly, when you have to discard, irrespective of who is leading, the discard of a high card from a suit indicates that you have some values in that suit.

You must, of course, be careful not to signal with higher cards than you can afford and so give up potential tricks but you should try to make your signals unmistakable. These high encouraging, low discouraging methods are fairly standard in bridge but there are numerous alternatives available that can be used by partnership agreement.

♠ A J 3
♡ K 5 2
◇ 9 8 6
♣ 9 8 5 3

Deal 71. You are East and hold this hand. Your left-hand opponent (South) opens 1◇ and the bidding goes:

South	North
1◇	1♠
1NT	3NT

Your partner (West) leads the ♡4 and dummy goes down:

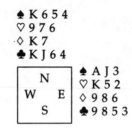

```
            ♠ K 6 5 4
            ♡ 9 7 6
            ◇ K 7
            ♣ K J 6 4
      ┌──────────┐   ♠ A J 3
      │    N     │   ♡ K 5 2
      │ W     E  │   ◇ 9 8 6
      │    S     │   ♣ 9 8 5 3
      └──────────┘
```

You win the first trick with the ♡K and return the ♡5 to partner's ♡10. Partner now plays ♡A, dropping declarer's ♡J, and continues with the ♡Q, on which everyone must discard. Dummy discards the ♣4. What do you discard?

With four tricks 'in the bag' your side needs one more to defeat the contract. The discard of a low club would discourage clubs and partner would have to choose between diamonds and spades. Similarly a low diamond would make partner choose between clubs and spades. Partner may choose wrongly and the only way to ensure a spade lead, if playing standard discards, is to discard the ♣J, a high card, clearly asking for a spade switch.

The full deal:

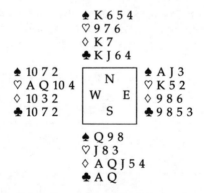

```
              ♠ K 6 5 4
              ♡ 9 7 6
              ◇ K 7
              ♣ K J 6 4
  ♠ 10 7 2   ┌──────────┐   ♠ A J 3
  ♡ A Q 10 4 │    N     │   ♡ K 5 2
  ◇ 10 3 2   │ W     E  │   ◇ 9 8 6
  ♣ 10 7 2   │    S     │   ♣ 9 8 5 3
             └──────────┘
              ♠ Q 9 8
              ♡ J 8 3
              ◇ A Q J 5 4
              ♣ A Q
```

The defence should thus take four heart tricks and the ♠A. A different discard from East would have put West to an awkward guess. When the hand was first played East actually discarded the ♣3, thus ensuring that his partner would make the wrong switch. West tried a club and declarer scooped up nine tricks in the minors.

♠ J 6 2   *Deal 72.* You are West and hold this hand. Your
♡ J 6 2   right-hand opponent (South) opens 1♣, North
◇ Q 6 4   responds 1◇ and South bids 3NT. What is your
♣ Q 10 8 5 opening lead?

Both minor suits have been bid by the opponents and you must choose between hearts and spades. Let us assume you try the ♠2. Dummy goes down:

♠ A 10 7
♡ A 10 7
◇ J 8 7 2
♣ 7 6 3

♠ J 6 2
♡ J 6 2
◇ Q 6 4
♣ Q 10 8 5

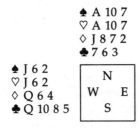

Dummy's ♠A wins the first trick, partner playing the ♠3. The ♣3 is led from dummy to declarer's ♣9 and your ♣10. What do you lead now?

Partner discouraged your spade lead so you must now try a heart (the ♡2), low from an honour again.

The full deal:

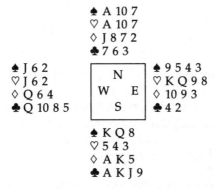

♠ A 10 7
♡ A 10 7
◇ J 8 7 2
♣ 7 6 3

♠ J 6 2   ♠ 9 5 4 3
♡ J 6 2   ♡ K Q 9 8
◇ Q 6 4   ◇ 10 9 3
♣ Q 10 8 5   ♣ 4 2

♠ K Q 8
♡ 5 4 3
◇ A K 5
♣ A K J 9

If dummy's ♡A is played, partner will encourage with the ♡9 so that you will know what to do when you next gain the lead with a minor suit queen. If dummy plays low on the heart lead, partner will play the ♡8 (he knows you have the ♡J) and will continue hearts from his side. Declarer can't avoid losing two hearts and three tricks in the minor suits.

Postscript: The hand has been arranged so that, from West's point of view, the major suits are identical, and he can only tell which is the best suit to continue by his partner's signals.

We have only considered the defence. Declarer would have done much better to play the ♣A-K and, if no honour fell, to switch to the ♢A-K and another diamond. Declarer will often get away with his actual line of play, however, if the defence has no system of signalling encouragement or discouragement of the suit led.

♠ 9 6 2
♡ 7 3
♢ Q 10 6 3 2
♣ K 8 4

Deal 73. You are East and hold this hand. Your left-hand opponent (South) opens 1♠ and the bidding goes:

	South	North
	1♠	2♣
	2♠	4♠

Your partner (West) leads the ♡K and dummy goes down:

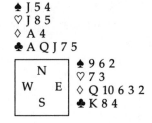

```
        ♠ J 5 4
        ♡ J 8 5
        ◇ A 4
        ♣ A Q J 7 5
    ┌─────────┐  ♠ 9 6 2
    │    N    │  ♡ 7 3
    │ W     E │  ◇ Q 10 6 3 2
    │    S    │  ♣ K 8 4
    └─────────┘
```

What do you think partner has led from and what do you play to the first trick?

You expect partner to try an attacking lead because the opponents are in a high level contract and have indicated that they have long suits. The defence must try to make its side suit winners before declarer discards losers on dummy's clubs. The lead of the ♡K denies the ♡A; partner can't have the ♡K-Q-J as you can see the ♡J in dummy but he will certainly have the ♡Q and there is the chance of another trick in the suit if you can get him to lead it again for you to ruff the third round. You must, therefore, encourage the heart lead by playing the ♡7.

The full deal:

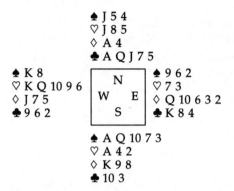

```
                          ♠ J 5 4
                          ♡ J 8 5
                          ◇ A 4
                          ♣ A Q J 7 5
    ♠ K 8                    ┌──────┐           ♠ 9 6 2
    ♡ K Q 10 9 6            │  N   │           ♡ 7 3
    ◇ J 7 5                 │ W  E │           ◇ Q 10 6 3 2
    ♣ 9 6 2                 │  S   │           ♣ K 8 4
                            └──────┘
                          ♠ A Q 10 7 3
                          ♡ A 4 2
                          ◇ K 9 8
                          ♣ 10 3
```

The play to the first trick is ♡K, ♡5, ♡7, ♡A. Declarer enters dummy with the ◇A and finesses a spade, losing to West's ♠K. West continues with the ♡Q and another heart for East to ruff. East can't be prevented from making his ♣K later so the contract goes one down.

Postscript: If, despite the spade fit, South plays in 3NT and West makes the same lead, East must play his ♡3 and leave West to decide if it's worth persisting with the suit.

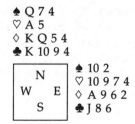

```
♠ 10 2          Deal 74. You are East and hold this hand. Your
♡ 10 9 7 4      left-hand opponent (South) opens 1♠ and the
◇ A 9 6 2       bidding goes:    South   North
♣ J 8 6                           1♠      2♣
                                  2♠      4♠
```

Your partner (West) leads the ◇10 and dummy goes down:

```
                          ♠ Q 7 4
                          ♡ A 5
                          ◇ K Q 5 4
                          ♣ K 10 9 4
                   ┌──────┐           ♠ 10 2
                   │  N   │           ♡ 10 9 7 4
                   │ W  E │           ◇ A 9 6 2
                   │  S   │           ♣ J 8 6
                   └──────┘
```

Dummy's ◊K is played on your partner's lead of ◊10. How do you defend?

The lead is very revealing. It can't be from a sequence such as ◊10-9-8 as you can see the ◊9 in your own hand. It is probably a short suit lead, made in the hope of obtaining a ruff. Can it be a singleton? It's unlikely that West should have precisely the singleton ◊10 and if he had, declarer would have had four diamonds and might well have rebid 2◊ over 2♣. It's more likely that West has led from ◊10-x and your defence should be based on this assumption.

Refuse to play your ◊A, therefore, but encourage with the ◊9.

The full deal:

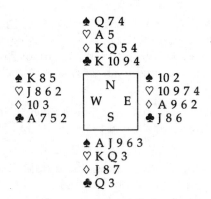

```
                    ♠ Q 7 4
                    ♡ A 5
                    ◊ K Q 5 4
                    ♣ K 10 9 4
    ♠ K 8 5                         ♠ 10 2
    ♡ J 8 6 2         N             ♡ 10 9 7 4
    ◊ 10 3       W        E         ◊ A 9 6 2
    ♣ A 7 5 2         S             ♣ J 8 6
                    ♠ A J 9 6 3
                    ♡ K Q 3
                    ◊ J 8 7
                    ♣ Q 3
```

The first trick is won with dummy's ◊K, East playing the ◊9. A spade is finessed to West's ♠K, West then leading a second diamond to East's ◊A, and a third round of diamonds is led for West to ruff. The ♣A must make later to defeat the contract.

Postscript: If East plays the ◊A on the first round (and returns a diamond) the contract will make, because when West makes his ♠K he can't put his partner back on lead to get his diamond ruff. It is almost as bad for East to play the ◊2 on the first trick as West would be deterred from continuing with the suit. The ◊9 ensures an accurate defence.

♠ 4
♡ 9 8 2
◊ A Q 2
♣ 9 7 6 5 4 3

Deal 75. You are East and hold this hand. The opponents bid as follows

South	North
1♠	3♠
4♠	

Your partner (West) makes the passive lead of ♠5 and dummy goes down:

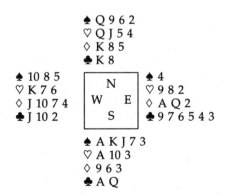

♠ Q 9 6 2
♡ Q J 5 4
◊ K 8 5
♣ K 8

♠ 4
♡ 9 8 2
◊ A Q 2
♣ 9 7 6 5 4 3

Declarer wins the first trick with the ♠J in hand and draws two more rounds of spades, ending in dummy. What are your two discards?

If partner can gain the lead you want a switch to diamonds but the ◊2 would be discouraging and you can't afford to discard the ◊Q. Fortunately you have two discards to make so you can first discourage clubs by discarding the ♣3 and then discourage hearts by playing the ♡2.

The full deal:

♠ Q 9 6 2
♡ Q J 5 4
◊ K 8 5
♣ K 8

♠ 10 8 5
♡ K 7 6
◊ J 10 7 4
♣ J 10 2

♠ 4
♡ 9 8 2
◊ A Q 2
♣ 9 7 6 5 4 3

♠ A K J 7 3
♡ A 10 3
◊ 9 6 3
♣ A Q

When partner gains the lead with his ♡K, having been warned not to lead a club or a heart, he will switch to ◊J. This will ensure three further tricks for the defence. If East fails to signal for a diamond lead, declarer has time to discard a losing diamond on dummy's fourth heart.

CHAPTER 16

Covering Honours and Discarding

Normally declarer plays low from one hand towards honour cards in the other hand and the defender who plays second to the trick usually plays low also. Sometimes, however, declarer leads an honour card and the defender who plays next has to decide whether to play a higher honour card on it.

Declarer's purpose in leading an honour is to try *to trap a defender's high card between honours in each hand.* For example:

$$♠ A x x x$$
$$♠ K x x \qquad ♠ 9 8 x$$
$$♠ Q J 10$$

Declarer (South) leads the ♠Q hoping to trap West's ♠K. In this example the ♠K is doomed whether West plays it now or not.

Declarer may not, in all cases, have such a solid suit. The position may be:

(a)   ♡ A x x x   (b)   ♡ A x x x
   ♡ K 10 x   ♡ 8 x x   or   ♡ K x x   ♡ 10 9 x
        ♡ Q J 9   ♡ Q J 8

Now if South leads the ♡Q and West plays the ♡K, the ♡A will be forced out, so setting up West's ♡10 in (a), East's ♡10 in (b). Thus, the purpose of covering an honour with an honour is *to promote a trick for your side.* If you see no chance of doing this you should play low.

Usually of course you can't see all four hands so you will have to judge whether to cover or not; here are some common situations to guide you:

1 Do not cover if there is no hope of setting up a trick for your side.
   Contract 4♠.

$$♠ A J 10 9 8$$
$$♠ K 3 2$$
$$♠ Q \text{ led}$$

When South (declarer) leads the ♠Q, West should not cover;
there is no hope of setting up a trick for his side as all the other
high cards are in dummy.

2 Do not cover if your high card cannot be trapped. Contract
   3NT.

$$◊ A x x$$
$$◊ K x x x$$
$$◊ Q \text{ led}$$

West should save his ◊K for the fourth round. The ◊A *has* to be
played by the third round.

3 Do not cover the first of touching honours. Contract 3NT.

$$♣ Q J 9 6$$
$$♣ 10 8 4 \qquad ♣ K 5 3$$
$$♣ A 7 2$$

If ♣Q is led from dummy, East should not cover the first time
because, after the ♣A has won, the opponents may finesse the
♣9 on the way back to dummy. East should cover the ♣J if this
is next led, to ensure that partner makes his ♣10.

4 It is often right to cover if you are short in a suit.

$$♠ A x x \qquad\qquad\qquad ♠ K x x$$
$$♠ K x \qquad \text{or} \qquad ♠ Q x$$
$$♠ Q \text{ led} \qquad\qquad\qquad ♠ J \text{ led}$$

You cover in each case because, unless you know otherwise,
your shortage in the suit will incline you to believe that partner
has some length, so it may be possible to set up tricks in his
hand. Also, if you play low, your honour will drop next time
even if South plays a low card.

5 It often pays to cover if there is more than one honour sitting
   over you.

$$♡ A Q x \qquad\qquad\qquad ♡ A Q J x$$
$$♡ K x x \qquad \text{or} \qquad ♡ K x x$$
$$♡ J \text{ led} \qquad\qquad\qquad ♡ 10 \text{ led}$$

On the first hand West would cover, hoping that East had the ♡10; on the second he would cover, hoping that East had ♡ 9-x-x-x.

6 There can be some difficult situations when a side suit is led in a trump contract. Imagine the contract is 4♠ in each case:

♡ A x		♡ A x x
♡ K x x	or	♡ K x x
♡ Q led		♡ Q led

On the first hand a sneaky declarer may lead the ♡Q from a holding such as ♡Q-x-x (lacking the ♡J). If you don't cover, and dummy has some trumps left, declarer will lose no tricks in the suit. Similarly on the second hand, declarer could be leading from ♡Q-x.

The examples given above should help you to come to the right decision on most hands but you will not always know whether to cover an honour card that is led from the closed hand, particularly if a side suit is led in a trump contract. You should try to anticipate the event when you are defending, so that you will not be caught in an agonising trance that gives the show away when the critical card is led.

Discards

The use of a discard as a defensive signal has already been described (p.152) but the subject of discards deserves a section of its own. There is no doubt that, by discarding the wrong cards, defenders throw away hundreds of points each time they play. Of course, it is sometimes impossible to make the right discards, for example if the opponents have caught you in a squeeze, but we are not concerned with that in this book. Although it is not easy to make rules about discards, a few general guidelines are listed below:

1 Always listen carefully to the opponents' bidding and try to get a mental picture of their hands.
2 Examine dummy closely to see if he is stronger or weaker than he should be and whether he has any previously undisclosed long suits.

3 Try to count declarer's points and his likely tricks.
4 Try to decide which suits partner can stop.
5 If possible keep at least four cards in the opponents' long suits. It is surprising how often a holding such as 9-x-x-x or even 8-x-x-x can provide a trick once a few honours have come crashing down on the early rounds of play. If you can keep only one such suit, keep the one that partner can't possibly stop.
6 If you have to find several discards, try to let go several cards of one suit, rather than picking away at several suits, spoiling your holding in each.
7 Try to keep an entry to partner's hand, if you think he has a winner.
8 Try to avoid being 'thrown in' with no safe card of exit.

♠ K 8 7 5   *Deal 76.* You are East and hold this hand. Your
♡ K 7   left-hand opponent (South) opens 1♡ and North
♢ A 10 9 4   responds 4♡.
♣ K 5 4

Your partner (West) leads the ♠J against 4♡ and dummy goes down:

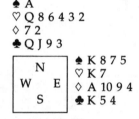

```
              ♠ A
              ♡ Q 8 6 4 3 2
              ♢ 7 2
              ♣ Q J 9 3
           ┌──────────┐   ♠ K 8 7 5
           │    N     │   ♡ K 7
           │ W     E  │   ♢ A 10 9 4
           │    S     │   ♣ K 5 4
           └──────────┘
```

Dummy's ♠A wins the first trick and the ♡Q is led from dummy. Do you cover?

The purpose of covering an honour with an honour is to set up a trick (or tricks) for your side. Quite often one does cover, if short in a suit, hoping to set up a trick in partner's hand. However, declarer has bid hearts, and must have at least four, so partner can have no more than a singleton. There is nothing to set up so play the ♡7 not the ♡K. Declarer may misguess and go up with the ♡A, hoping to drop the singleton ♡K from West.

Later in the hand dummy's ♣Q is led. Do you cover? No, you should not cover the first card of a run. Play low, and if the ♣J is led to the next trick, cover that. If the ♣3 or ♣9 is led to the next round, play low.

The full deal:

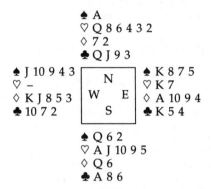

```
                    ♠ A
                    ♡ Q 8 6 4 3 2
                    ◇ 7 2
                    ♣ Q J 9 3
    ♠ J 10 9 4 3      ┌─────┐      ♠ K 8 7 5
    ♡ –               │  N  │      ♡ K 7
    ◇ K J 8 5 3     W │     │ E    ◇ A 10 9 4
    ♣ 10 7 2          │  S  │      ♣ K 5 4
                      └─────┘
                    ♠ Q 6 2
                    ♡ A J 10 9 5
                    ◇ Q 6
                    ♣ A 8 6
```

If you cover the ♣Q, declarer will win with the ♣A and then lead the ♣6 and finesse the ♣9, so taking four tricks in the suit. Holding up the ♣K until the ♣J is played ensures one trick for the defence. With a possible heart trick as well, and two diamonds, you have a chance of defeating the contract.

♠ K 6 2   *Deal 77.* You are West and hold this hand. Your
♡ K 10 5 2   right-hand opponent (South) opens 1NT (12-14
◇ 10 9 8 3   points) and the bidding goes:

	South	North
♣ Q 4	1NT	2♣
	2♠	3NT

What is your opening lead?

North's Stayman enquiry must have been based on a heart suit, and South has bid spades, so you must choose a minor suit lead. The ◇10 is an obvious choice as the top of a sequence lead is much more attractive than the lead from a doubleton honour.

You (West) lead the ◇10 against 3NT by South and dummy goes down:

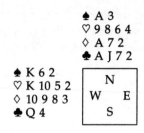

```
            ♠ A 3
            ♡ 9 8 6 4
            ◇ A 7 2
            ♣ A J 7 2
♠ K 6 2        N
♡ K 10 5 2
◇ 10 9 8 3   W     E
♣ Q 4          S
```

Declarer wins the first trick in his own hand with the ◇K and leads the ♠Q. Do you cover?

Later in the play declarer leads the ♣10. Do you cover?

You should not cover the ♠Q because the ♠A will have to be played on the second round and your ♠K will make later. You must cover the ♣10 because you are short in clubs and two honours sit over you.

The full deal:

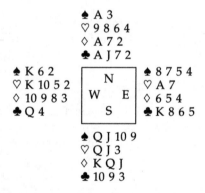

```
              ♠ A 3
              ♡ 9 8 6 4
              ◇ A 7 2
              ♣ A J 7 2
♠ K 6 2          N          ♠ 8 7 5 4
♡ K 10 5 2                  ♡ A 7
◇ 10 9 8 3    W     E       ◇ 6 5 4
♣ Q 4            S          ♣ K 8 6 5
              ♠ Q J 10 9
              ♡ Q J 3
              ◇ K Q J
              ♣ 10 9 3
```

By covering the ♣10 you restrict declarer to two tricks in the suit but, if you fail to cover, he will make three tricks by leading the ♣3 next time.

Declarer might have chosen other ways to play this hand but if he does play on the black suits, careful defence will restrict him to eight tricks.

♠ Q 10 5 2   *Deal 78.* You are East and hold this hand. Your
♡ 10 9 3   left-hand opponent (South) opens 1◊ and the
◊ A 6 4   bidding goes:

	South	North
	1◊	1♠
	1NT	3NT

♣ Q 10 6

South's rebid shows 15-16 points and North could raise to 3NT on 10-15 points (possibly even 16 points). Your partner will be weak and short of entries, so he will not necessarily lead his longest suit. He leads the ♠8 against 3NT by South and dummy goes down:

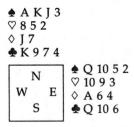

          ♠ A K J 3
          ♡ 8 5 2
          ◊ J 7
          ♣ K 9 7 4

                    ♠ Q 10 5 2
    N   ♡ 10 9 3
W   E   ◊ A 6 4
    S   ♣ Q 10 6

Dummy wins with the ♠A and you encourage with the ♠5. The ♣4 is led, you play the ♣6 and South wins with the ♣J. South now leads the ♣A. Play the ♣Q. Declarer knows you have it and it will fall on the next round anyway. Your only hope is to persuade declarer that you started with ♣Q-6 only. He may now lead a low club to the ♣9, believing that your partner has the ♣10.

The full deal:

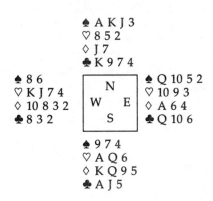

          ♠ A K J 3
          ♡ 8 5 2
          ◊ J 7
          ♣ K 9 7 4

♠ 8 6   ♠ Q 10 5 2
♡ K J 7 4   N   ♡ 10 9 3
◊ 10 8 3 2 W   E ◊ A 6 4
♣ 8 3 2   S   ♣ Q 10 6

          ♠ 9 7 4
          ♡ A Q 6
          ◊ K Q 9 5
          ♣ A J 5

If your ploy succeeds you will win the third club trick and can lead the ♡10 (through strength to weakness) to give the defence the best chance of beating the contract. Incidentally, you will earn yourself the reputation of being a highly dangerous defender!

Postscript: If the opponents know you have a specific card and you know it can't take a trick, play it early.

♠ Q 8 7   *Deal 79.* You are East and hold this hand. Your
♡ 10 9 7   left-hand opponent (South) opens 2NT and North
◊ 7 6 2   raises to 6NT.
♣ Q 9 8 7

Your partner (West) leads the ♠J against 6NT by South and dummy goes down:

♠ 4 3
♡ K Q 8
◊ A 10 8 4
♣ K J 3 2

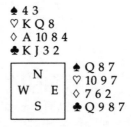

♠ Q 8 7
♡ 10 9 7
◊ 7 6 2
♣ Q 9 8 7

Dummy plays ♣3, you encourage with ♣8 and South wins with ♣A. He now plays off all his red suit winners (four diamonds and three hearts). Which five cards do you keep?

Declarer must have the ♣A and at least one other club for his bid. If you throw a club you may still make your ♣Q but one of dummy's low clubs will become established for an extra trick. You should, therefore, keep four clubs and a spade. The problem is that, if you keep the ♠Q, declarer can play a low spade and you will be thrown in, with nothing but clubs to lead towards dummy's ♣K-J-3-2. You must keep the ♠7 and throw the ♠Q, trusting that partner has the ♠10, as indicated by his lead.

The full deal:

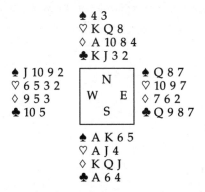

```
                      ♠ 4 3
                      ♡ K Q 8
                      ◊ A 10 8 4
                      ♣ K J 3 2
    ♠ J 10 9 2      ┌─────────┐      ♠ Q 8 7
    ♡ 6 5 3 2       │    N    │      ♡ 10 9 7
    ◊ 9 5 3         │ W     E │      ◊ 7 6 2
    ♣ 10 5          │    S    │      ♣ Q 9 8 7
                    └─────────┘
                      ♠ A K 6 5
                      ♡ A J 4
                      ◊ K Q J
                      ♣ A 6 4
```

With eleven tricks on top, declarer was just searching for his twelfth trick. If you had discarded a club or allowed yourself to be thrown in with the ♣Q you would have given him an easy path to his contract.

♠ Q J 10 4 2   *Deal 80*. You are West and hold this hand. Your
♡ Q 7 3   right-hand opponent (South) opens 2NT, North
◊ 6 2   responds 4NT and, after some thought, South
♣ 9 8 2   bids 6NT.

There is no problem with the opening lead. The ♠Q is the obvious card (top of a sequence). Dummy goes down:

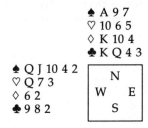

```
                      ♠ A 9 7
                      ♡ 10 6 5
                      ◊ K 10 4
                      ♣ K Q 4 3
    ♠ Q J 10 4 2    ┌─────────┐
    ♡ Q 7 3         │    N    │
    ◊ 6 2           │ W     E │
    ♣ 9 8 2         │    S    │
                    └─────────┘
```

Declarer ducks the first spade and, on the second round, wins your ♠J with his ♠K. He now plays four rounds of clubs, ♣K, ♣Q from dummy and ♣A, ♣J from his own hand. What do you discard?

It looks easy. You need keep only two spades, so should you

discard your spare ♠2? No, this could be fatal, as it tells your partner nothing about your hand and he is in desperate trouble (see below).

The full deal:

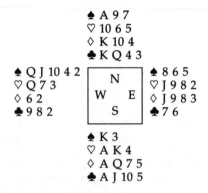

```
                    ♠ A 9 7
                    ♡ 10 6 5
                    ◇ K 10 4
                    ♣ K Q 4 3
  ♠ Q J 10 4 2                      ♠ 8 6 5
  ♡ Q 7 3          N                ♡ J 9 8 2
  ◇ 6 2        W       E            ◇ J 9 8 3
  ♣ 9 8 2          S                ♣ 7 6
                    ♠ K 3
                    ♡ A K 4
                    ◇ A Q 7 5
                    ♣ A J 10 5
```

On the third club, East can discard his last spade but on the fourth club he has to choose between the red suits, and he needs to know which red suit West can stop. Although West can't afford to discard a high heart, he *can* discard a low diamond to show his diamond weakness. East can now discard a heart, trusting his partner for that suit, and retaining the diamonds himself.

Postscript: The opponents have missed their club fit on the hand but it is up to East-West to defeat the actual contract. If West had discarded a 'lazy' spade on the fourth club, East might have guessed wrongly and discarded a diamond, giving declarer his twelfth trick. Bridge is a partnership game.

The Odds of how Missing Cards Divide

No of cards missing	Split	%
7	4-3	62.2
	5-2	30.5
	6-1	6.8
	7-0	0.5
6	4-2	48.5
	3-3	35.5
	5-1	14.5
	6-0	1.5
5	3-2	67.8
	4-1	28.3
	5-0	3.9
4	3-1	49.7
	2-2	40.7
	4-0	9.6
3	2-1	78.0
	3-0	22.0
2	1-1	52.0
	2-0	48.0

An even number of missing cards is unlikely to split evenly, for example, a 3-3 split is less common than 4-2. An odd number of missing cards is likely to split as evenly as possible, for example 7 cards will probably split 4-3, 5 cards will probably split 3-2.

Index